KB270503

점프 업 파닉스 Jump Up Phonics 2 개정판

점프 업 파닉스 2 [개정판]

2008년 05월 20일 초판 1쇄 발행
2025년 04월 15일 개정 1쇄 발행

지은이 문호준/국제어학연구소 영어학부
그림 이경택
펴낸이 이규인
펴낸곳 국제어학연구소 출판부
출판등록 2010년 1월 18일 제302-2010-000006호
주소 서울특별시 마포구 대흥로4길 49, 1층(용강동 월명빌딩)
Tel (02) 704-0900 **팩시밀리** (02) 703-5117
홈페이지 www.bookcamp.co.kr
e-mail changbook1@hanmail.net
ISBN 979-11-9880103-6 13740
정가 18,000원

Jump Up Phonics 2

개정판

글 문호준·국제어학연구소 영어학부

국제어학연구소

CONTENTS

Unit 1 Short Vowel **a**

A rat is in the pan.
The rat eats bread with jam.
A man eats ham.
And he takes a nap on the mat.

Listen and repeat.

 and  ······▶  

 and  ······▶  

and  ······▶  

and  ······▶ 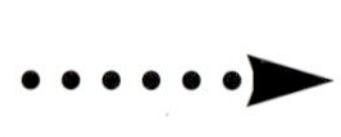 

  *ham*  

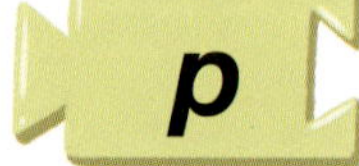  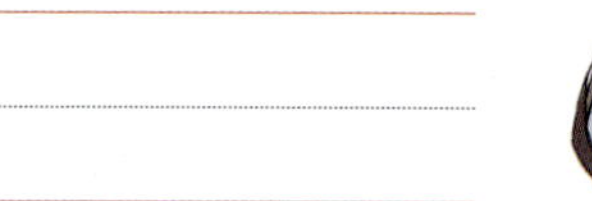 

  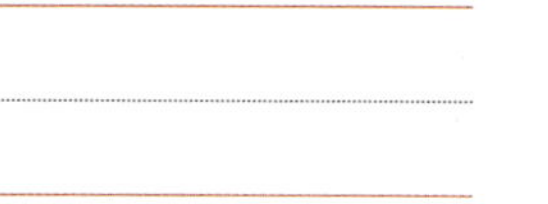 

8

Listen, point and repeat.

ham	 jam	 ram
 man	 pan	van
 nap	cap	 lap
 mat	 rat	 fat
 dad	 bad	 sad

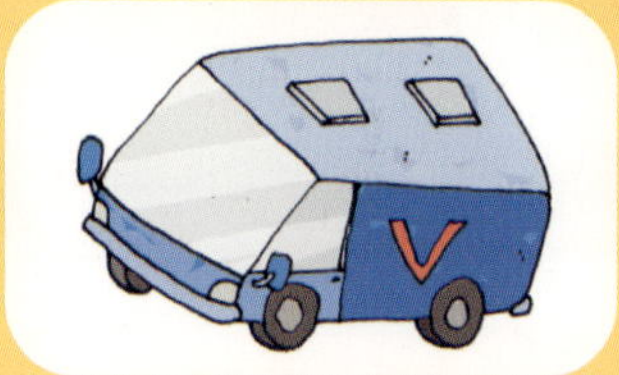

Sort the words according to the rhyme.

r	p	c
m	d	j
l	f	b

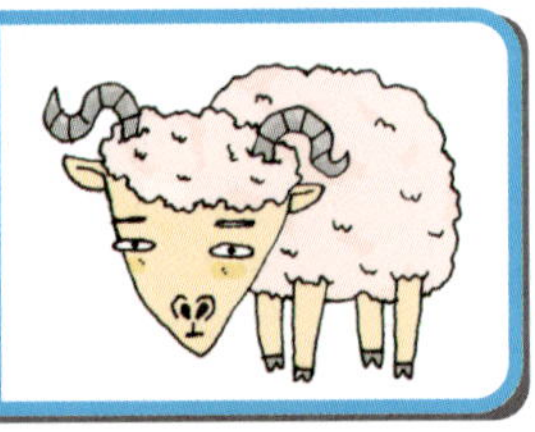

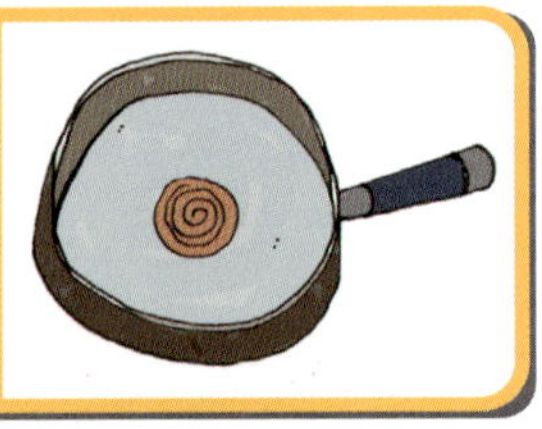

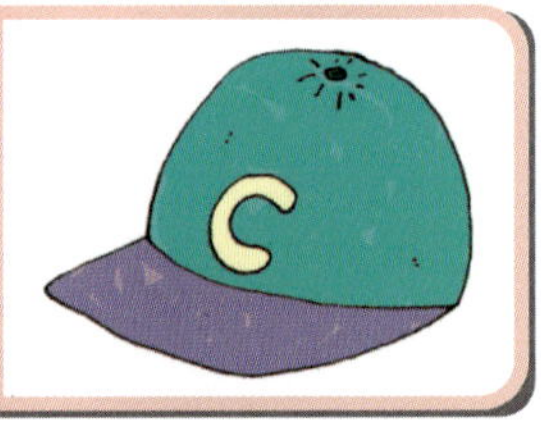

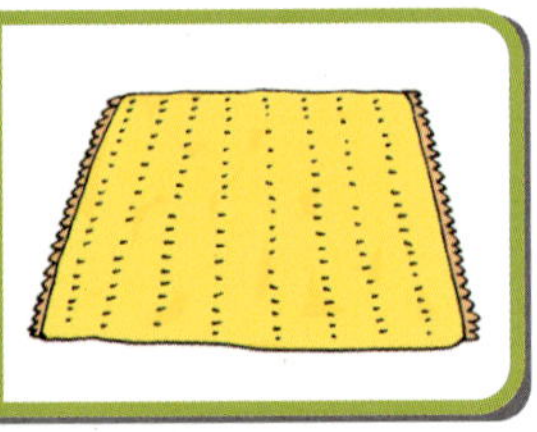

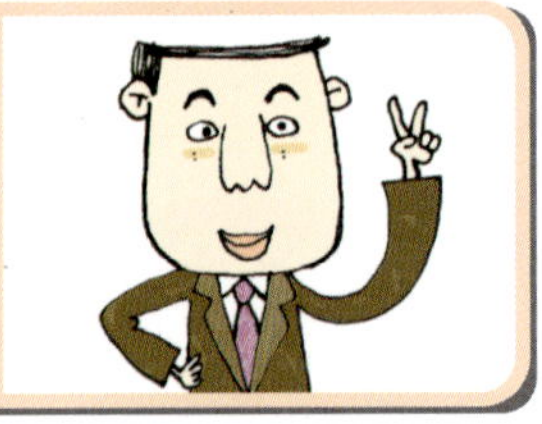

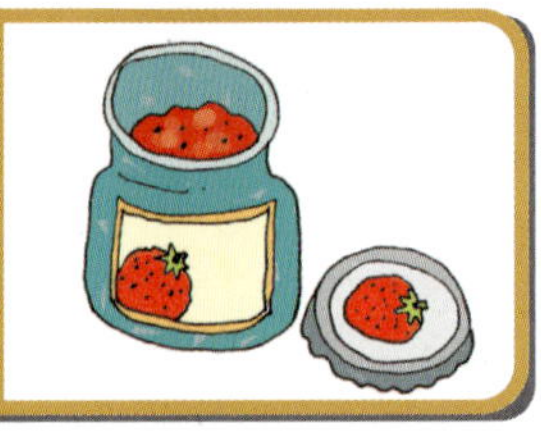

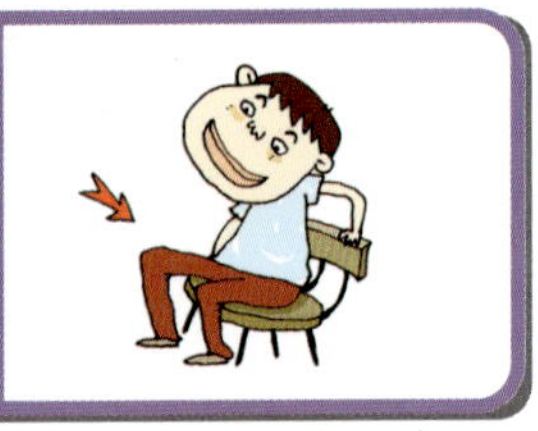

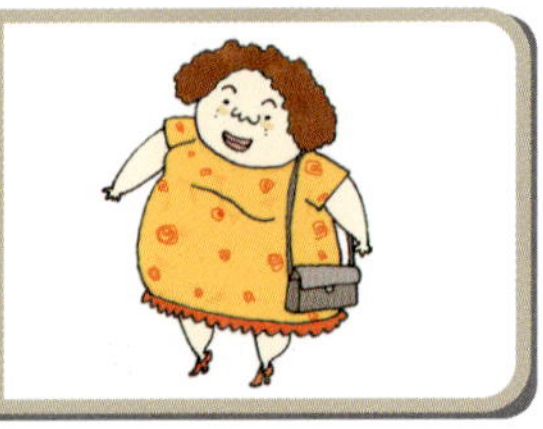

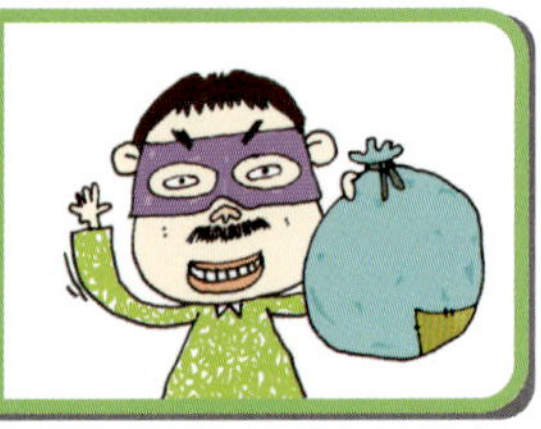

① _am

ram

② _at

③ _ap

④ _an

⑤ _ad

Listen and circle.

Read the sentence and check the T or F.

T   F

1

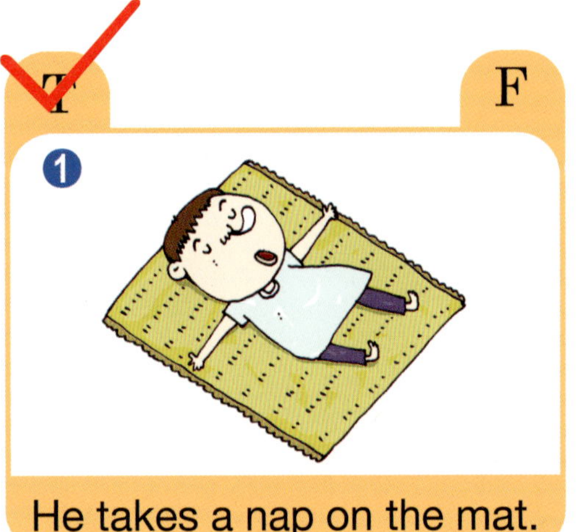

He takes a nap on the mat.

T   F

2

A ram is in the van.

T   F

3

The girl is fat.

T   F

4

A rat is in the pan.

T   F

5

Dad is sad.

T   F

6

A man eats ham.

Write and color.

ham   nap   mat   van   rat   cap   pan   ram   jam

1. ram

2.

3.

4.

5.

6.

7.

8.

9.

Circle the words and complete the story.

- A __rat__ is in the __________ .

- The __________ eats bread with __________ .

- A __________ eats __________ .

- And he takes a __________ on the __________ .

Activity *chant*

A fat rat is in the cap.
Where? Where? Where is the man?,
On the mat. On the mat.
He takes a nap.

She eats bread with jam.
Who? Who? Who eats ham?
A ram. A ram.
A ram is on the lap.

He drives a van.
What? What? What is in the van?
A pan. A pan.
A pan is in the van.

Unit 2 Short Vowel e

Ten eggs are on the bed.
The red hen finds the eggs.
The bad men have the eggs.
The red hen is sad.

Sounds

Listen and repeat.

 **e** and  **d** ·······▶  **ed**

 **e** and  **g** ·······▶  **eg**

 **e** and  **n** ·······▶  **en**

 **e** and  **t** ·······▶  **et**

 **b**  **ed** _____________ 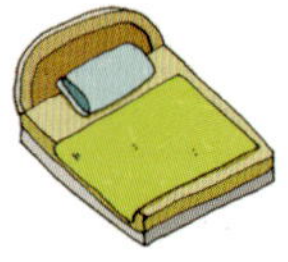

 **l**  **eg** _____________ 

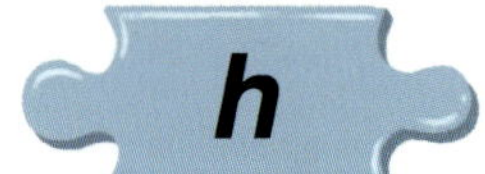 **h**  **en** _____________ 

 **n**  **et** _____________ 

Listen, point and repeat.

b**e**d	r**e**d	w**e**d
l**e**g	**e**gg	t**e**n
h**e**n	p**e**n	m**e**n
n**e**t	j**e**t	w**e**t

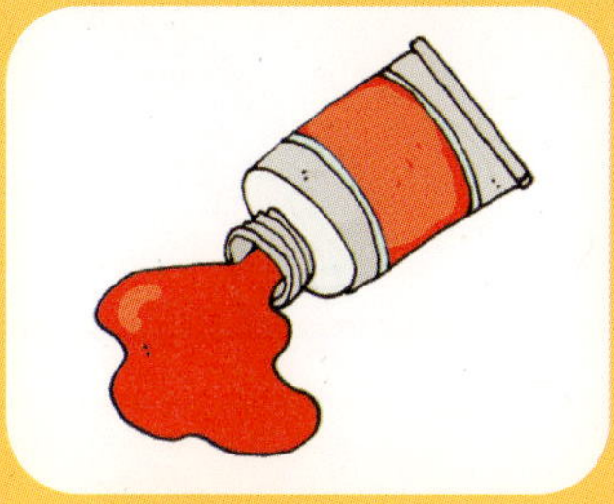

Sort the words according to the rhyme.

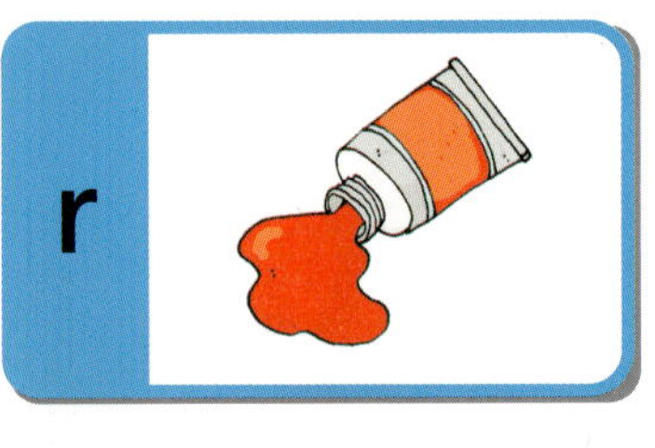 r

 p

 e

 h

 w

 j

 w

 l

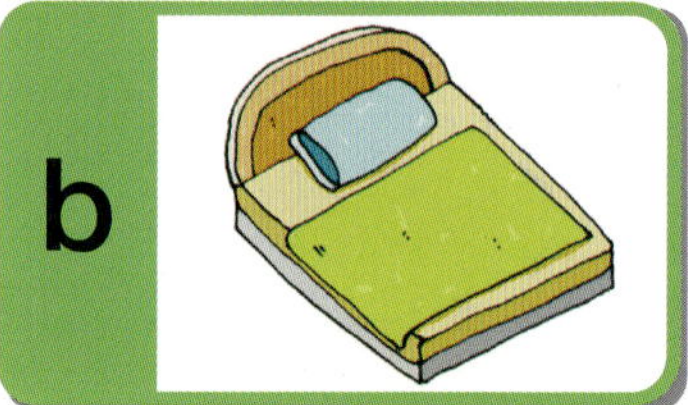 b

Listen and circle.

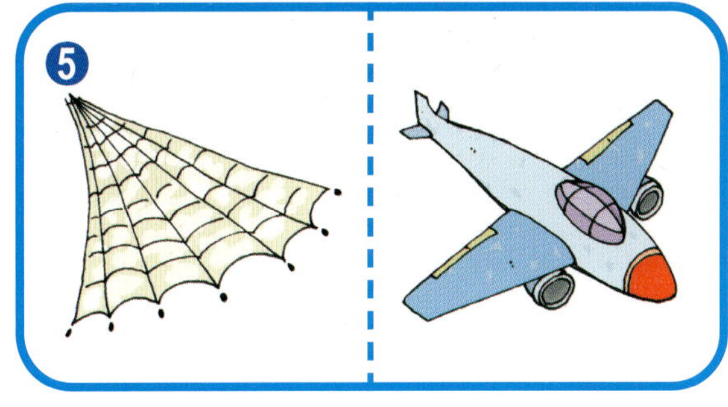

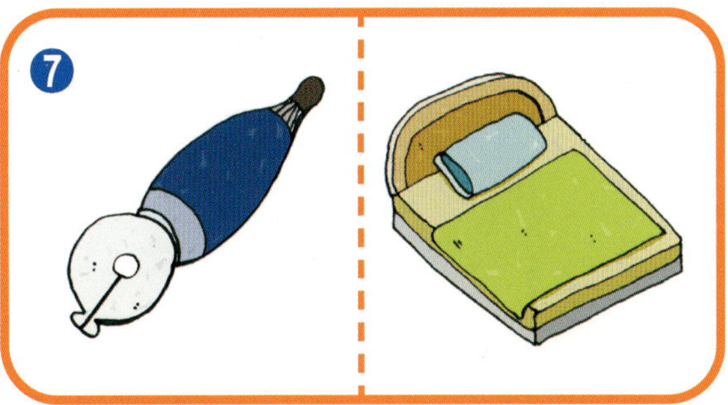

Read the sentence and check the T or F.

T   F

1

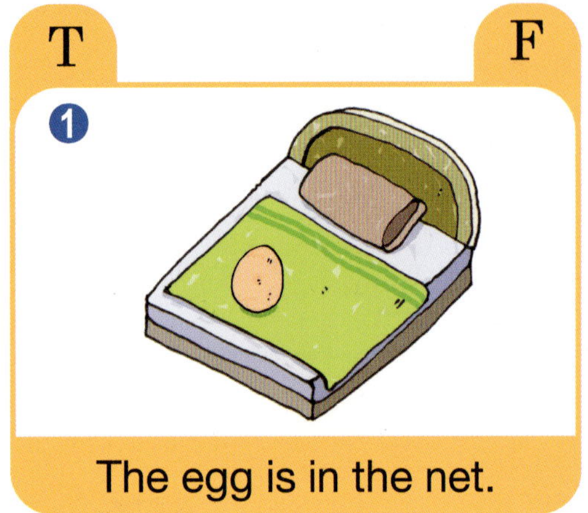

The egg is in the net.

T   F

2

The men have legs.

T   F

3

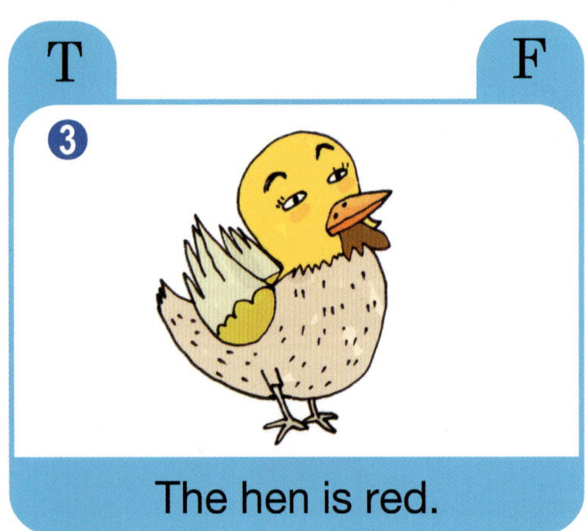

The hen is red.

T   F

4

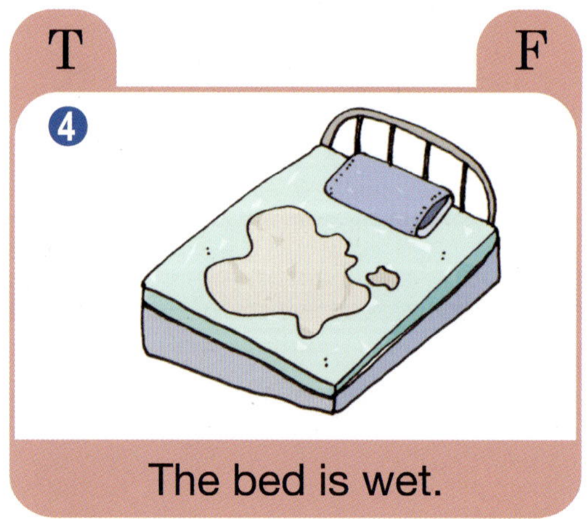

The bed is wet.

T   F

5

The cat has a jet.

T   F

6

A man has ten pens.

Write and color.

| egg | net | pen | bed | jet | ten | hen | leg | red |

Word Search

Circle the words and complete the story.

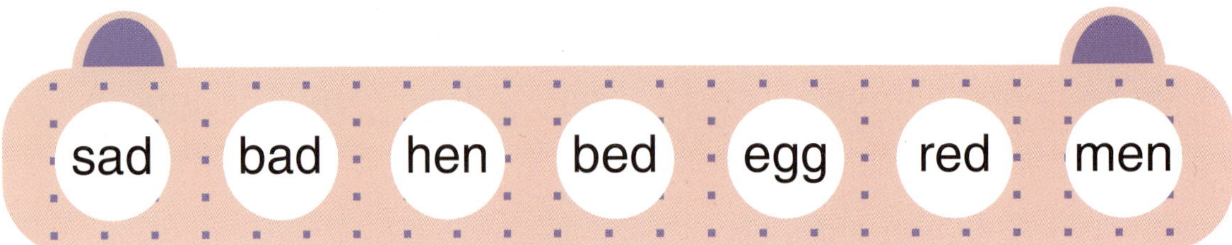

- Ten _________ s are on the bed.

- The _________ _________ finds the eggs.

- The _________ _________ have the eggs.

- The _________ _________ is sad.

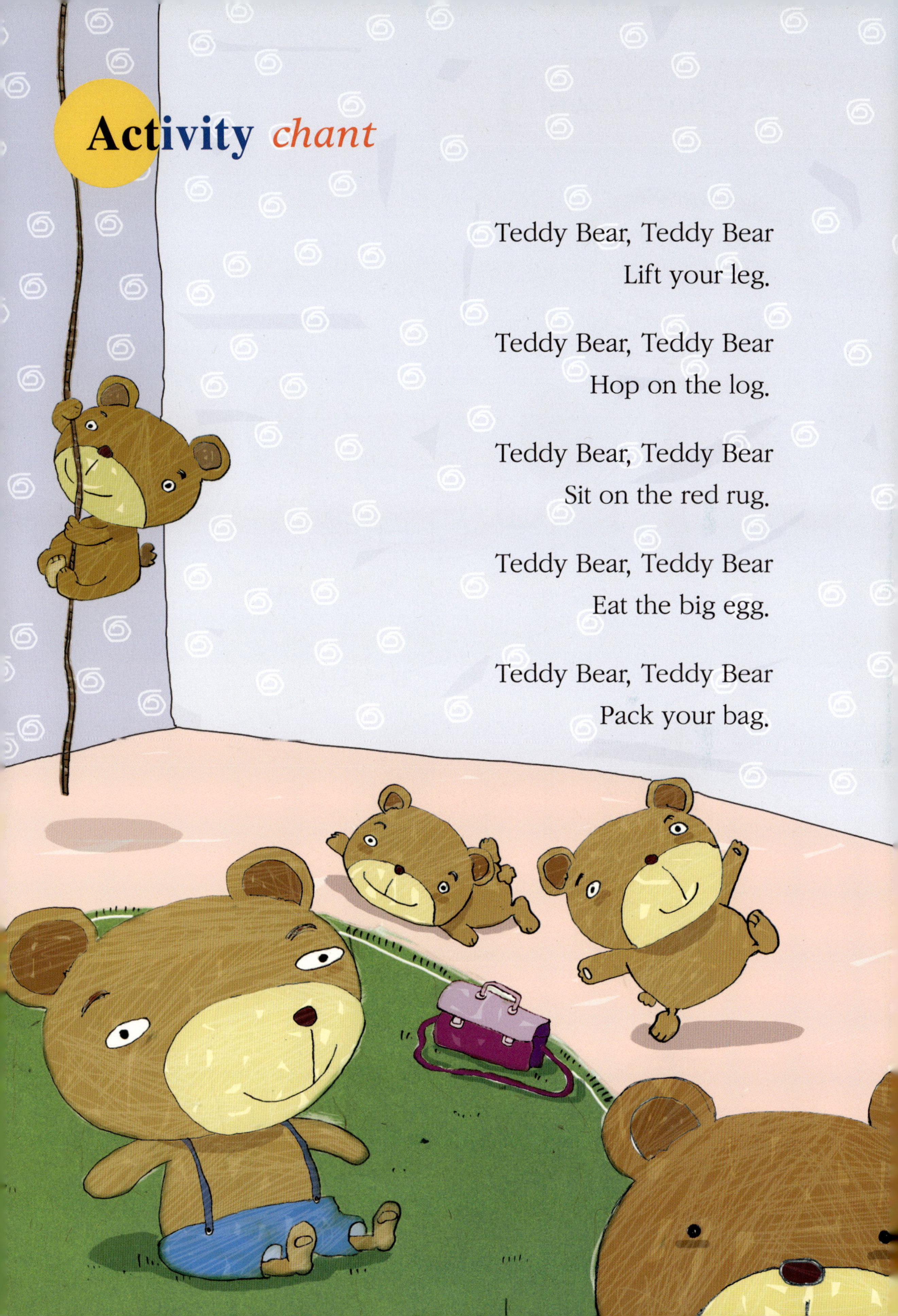

Activity chant

Teddy Bear, Teddy Bear
Lift your leg.

Teddy Bear, Teddy Bear
Hop on the log.

Teddy Bear, Teddy Bear
Sit on the red rug.

Teddy Bear, Teddy Bear
Eat the big egg.

Teddy Bear, Teddy Bear
Pack your bag.

The kid has a pig and a fish.
The pig has big lips.
The fish has a big fin.
The kid gives them a big hug.

Listen and repeat.

 and  ......➤ 

 and  ......➤ 

 and  ......➤ 

 and  ......➤ 

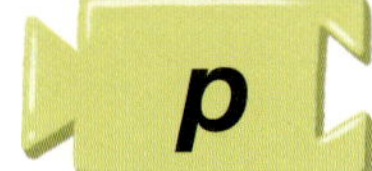  

Listen, point and repeat.

bib	 kid	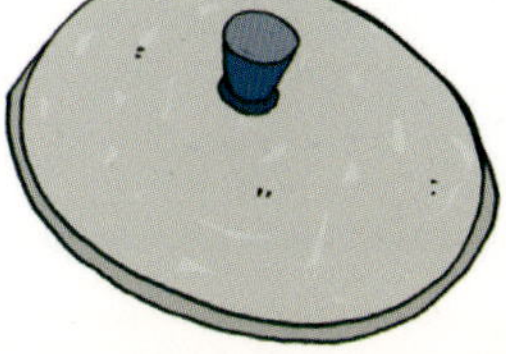 lid
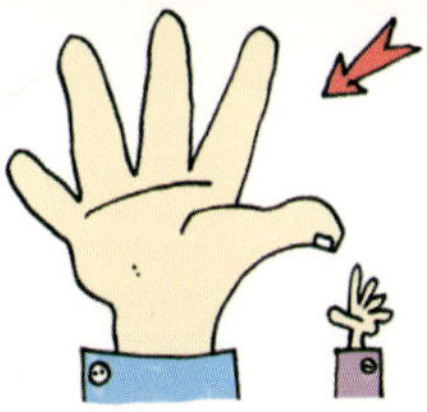 big	 pig	 pin
 fin	 sit	 hit
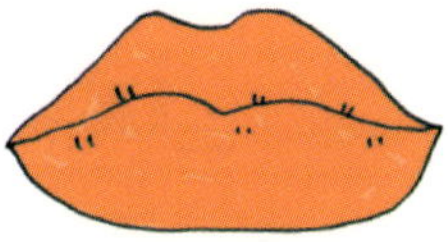 lip	 fish	 six

Sort the words according to the rhyme.

s	h	k
p	p	l
f	s	b

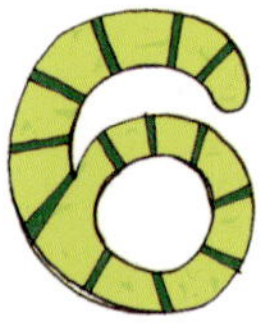

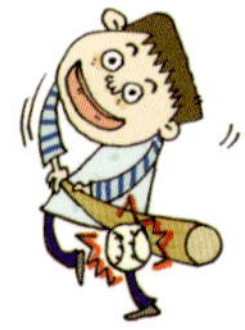

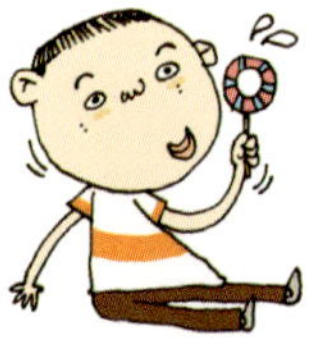

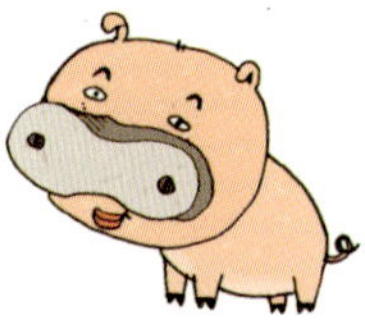

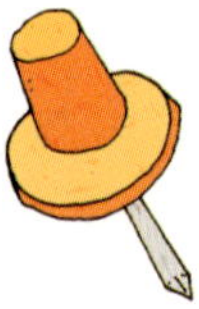

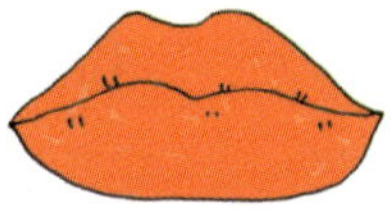

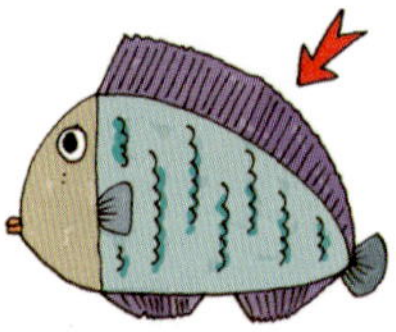

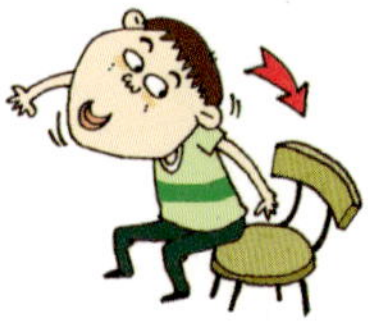

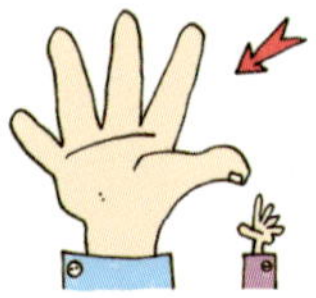

Listen and circle.

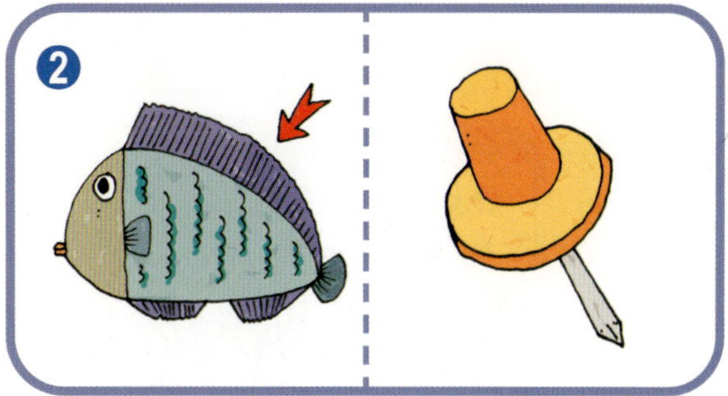

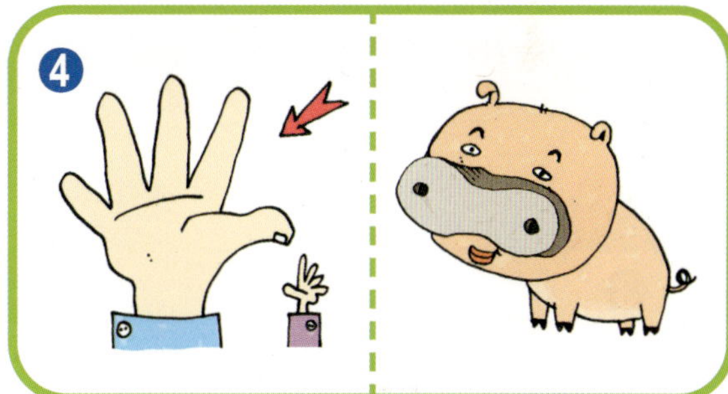

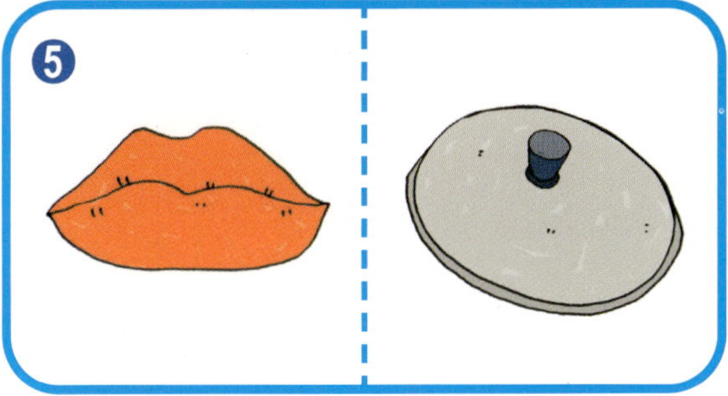

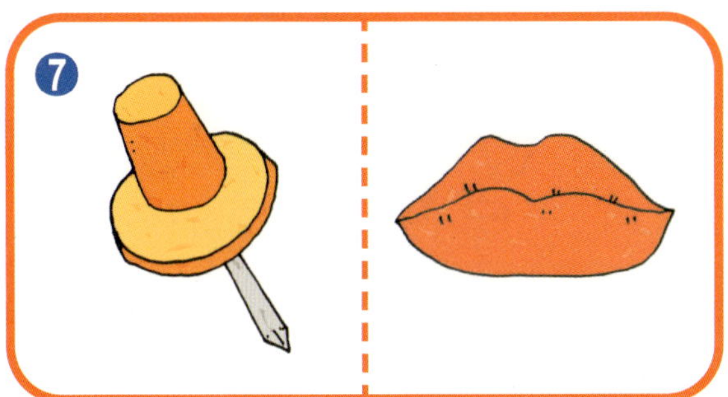

Practice – Read

Read the sentence and check the T or F.

T   F

1
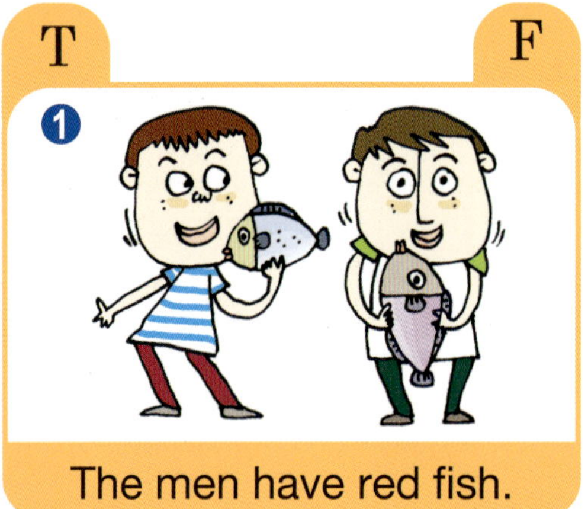
The men have red fish.

T   F

2
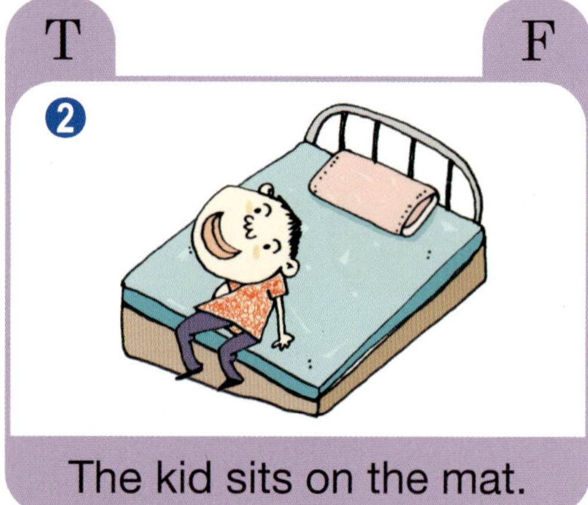
The kid sits on the mat.

T   F

3
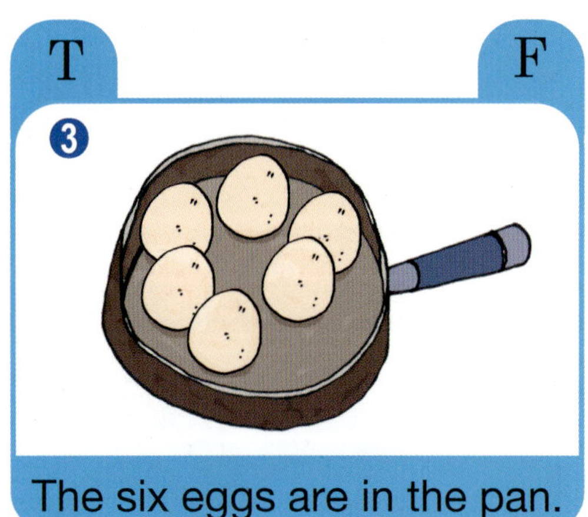
The six eggs are in the pan.

T   F

4
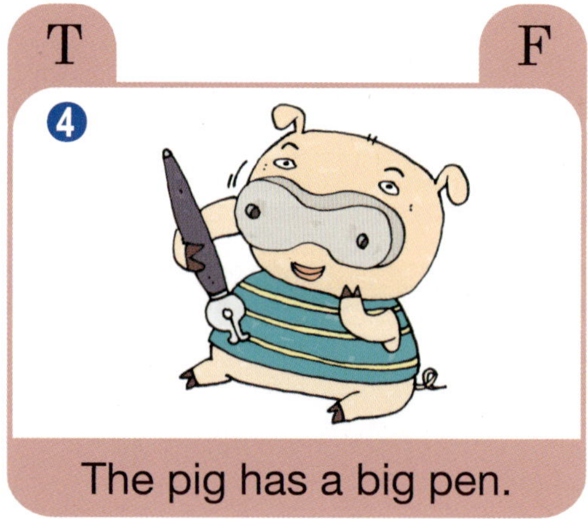
The pig has a big pen.

T   F

5
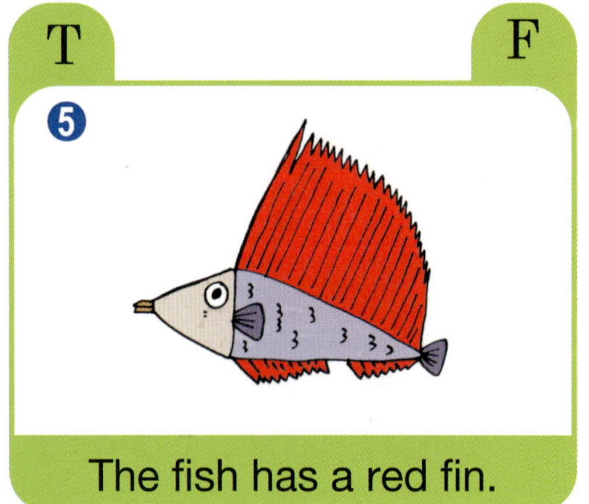
The fish has a red fin.

T   F

6
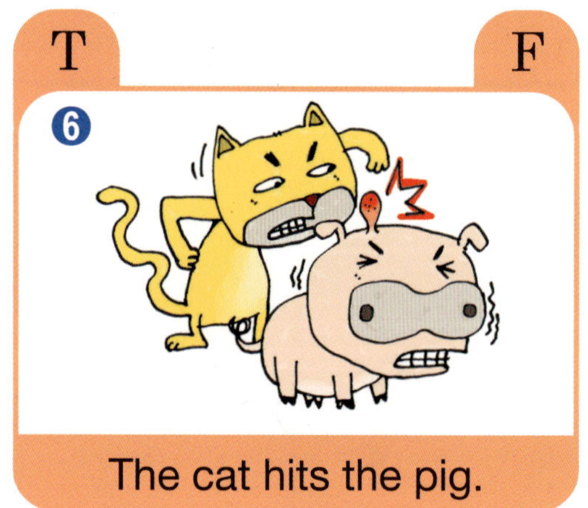
The cat hits the pig.

Write and color.

bib   sit   six   pig   big   fish   lip   kid   lid

1 

2 

3 

4 

5 

6 

7 

8 

9 

Circle the words and complete the story.

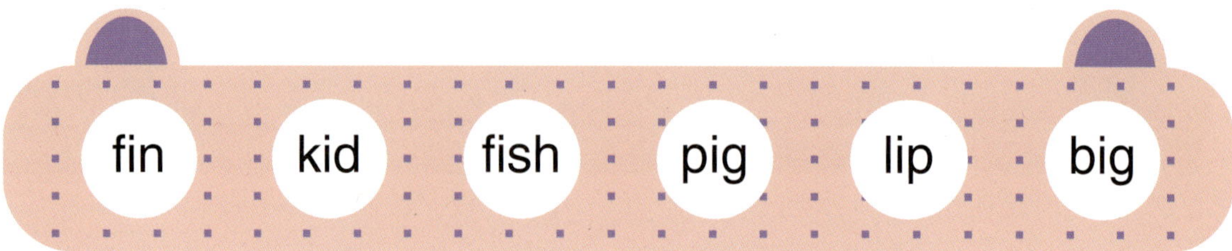

- The __________ has a __________ and a __________ .

- The __________ has __________ __________ s.

- The __________ has a __________ __________ .

- The __________ gives them a __________ hug.

The little kid has a bat.
Hit hit, hit the ball!

The big pig has a net.
Catch catch, catch the fish!

The fat rat has a jet.
Fly fly, fly in the sky!

A dog and a fox
like hopping on the log.
The dog is hopping with a top.
The fox is hopping with a pot.
They are so hot.

Sounds

Listen and repeat.

 o and  b ······▶  ob

 o and  d ······▶  od

 o and  g ······▶  og

 o and  p ······▶  op

 r  ob _______________ 

 n  od _______________ 

 d  og _______________ 

 t  op _______________ 

38

Listen, point and repeat.

rob	 hot	 pot
 dog	 jog	 log
 top	 mop	 hop
 nod	 box	 fox

Sort the words according to the rhyme.

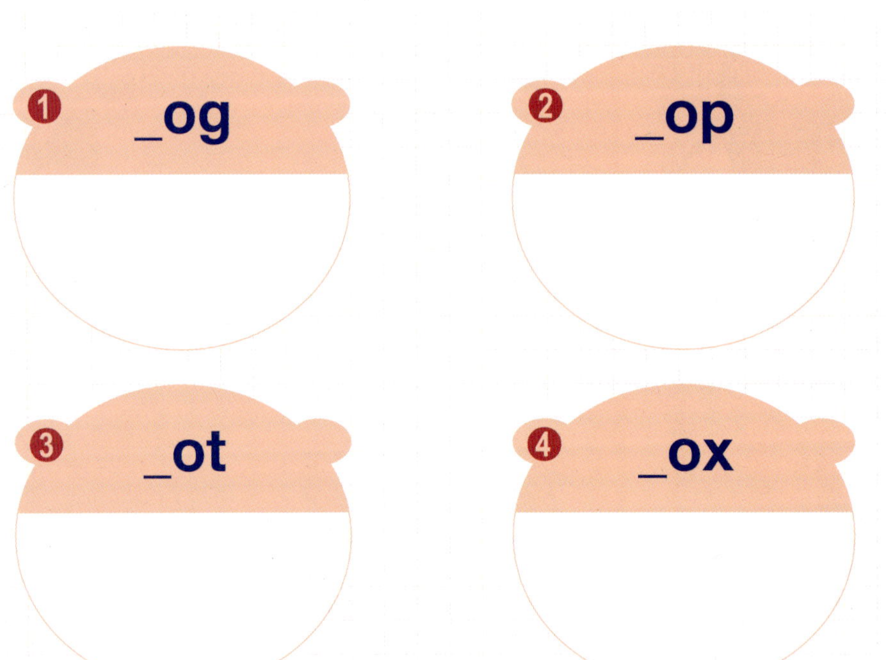

Listen and circle.

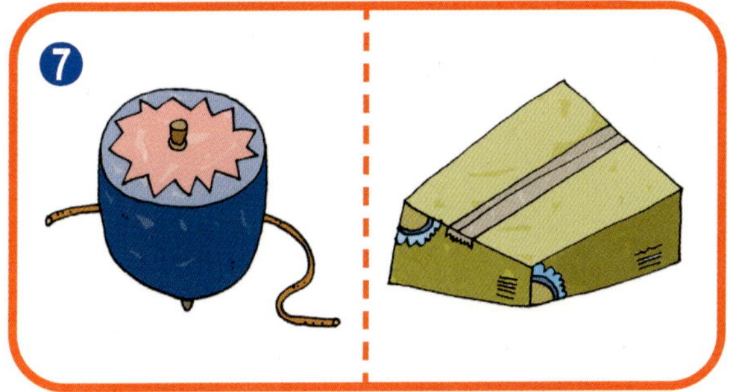

Read the sentence and check the T or F.

T   F

1 

The fox has a hot pot.

T   F

2 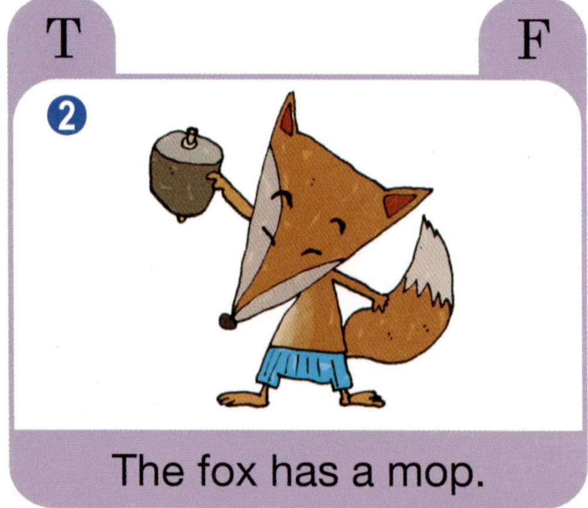

The fox has a mop.

T   F

3 

The dog is hot.

T   F

4 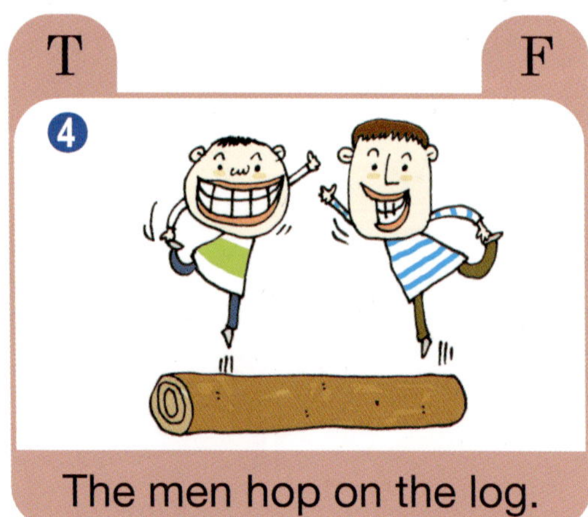

The men hop on the log.

T   F

5 

The fox is in the box.

T   F

6 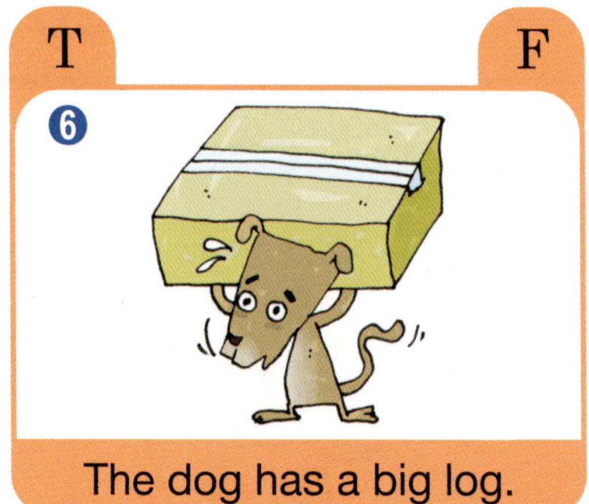

The dog has a big log.

Write and color.

fox   hot   log   dog   top   box   pot   jog   nod

1 

2 

3 

4 

5 

6 

7 

8 

9 

Circle the words and complete the story.

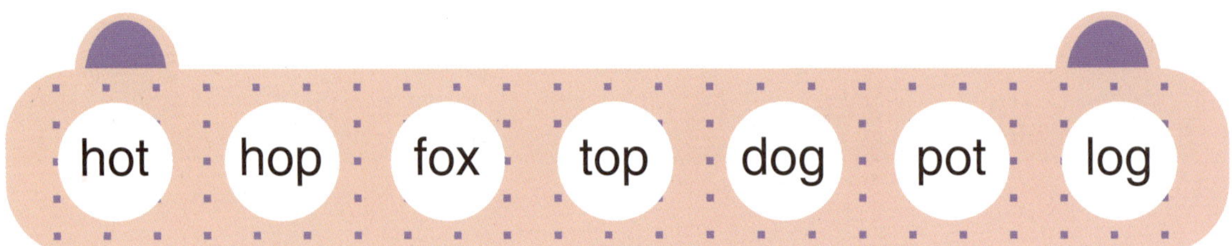

- A ______ and a ______ like ______ ping on the log.

- The ______ is ______ ping with a ______.

- The ______ is ______ ping with a ______.

- They are so ______.

Ac**tivity** *chant*

The fox cleans, cleans with a mop!

The dog plays, plays with a top!

The ox jogs, jogs with a cap!

The cat cooks, cooks with a pot!

Unit 5 Short Vowel u

A pup has nuts and buns.
The pup runs to the hut.
Oh! The pup drops nuts
and buns in the mud.
What a pity!

Listen and repeat.

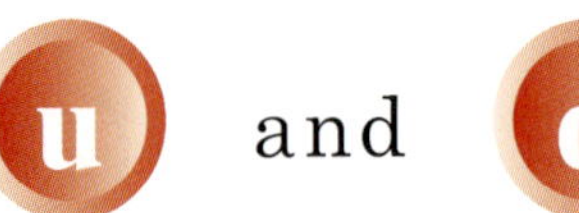  

u and d ·····▶ ud

 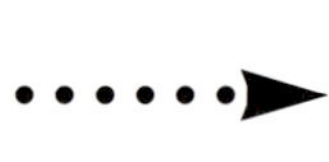 

u and g ·····▶ ug

u and m ·····▶ um

 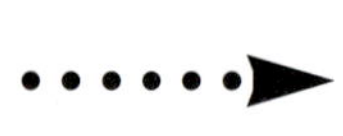 

u and n ·····▶ un

  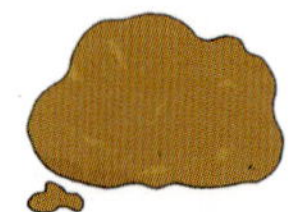

m   ud

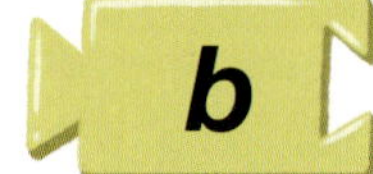  

b   ug

g   um

s   un

Listen, point and repeat.

bug	hug	rug
mug	mud	gum
bun	run	sun
up	cup	pup
cut	hut	nut

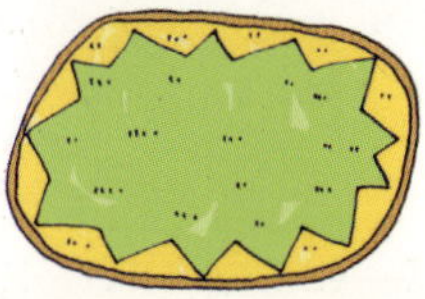

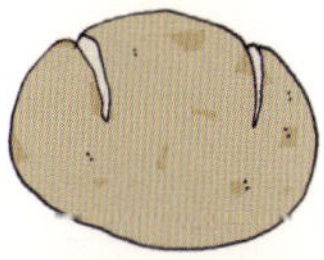

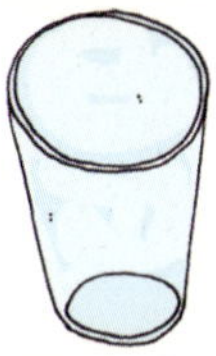

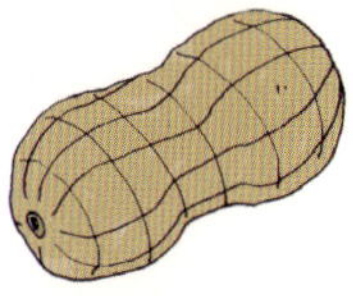

Sort the words according to the rhyme.

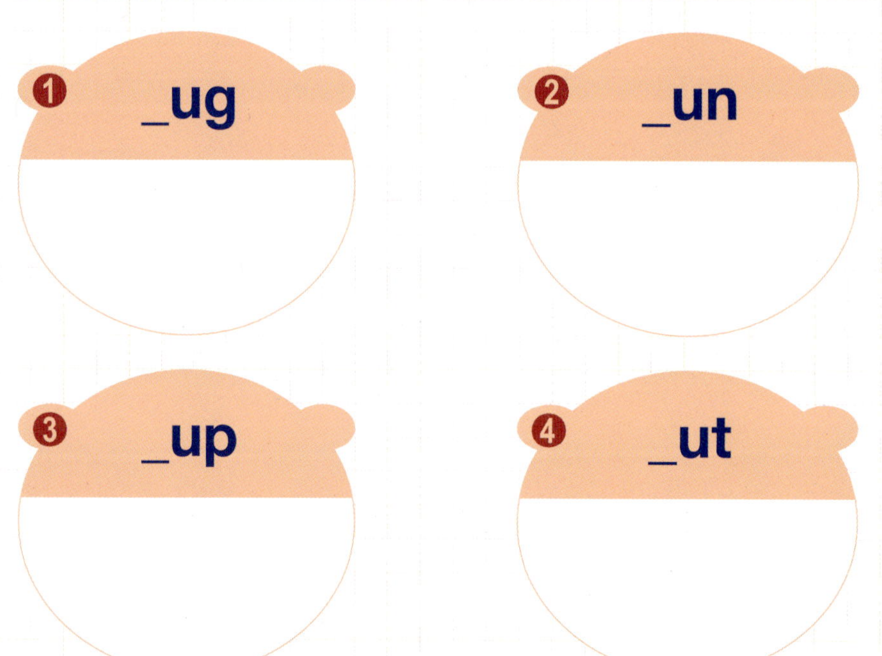

Listen and circle.

Read the sentence and check the T or F.

T   F

1

The pup has a mug.

T   F

2

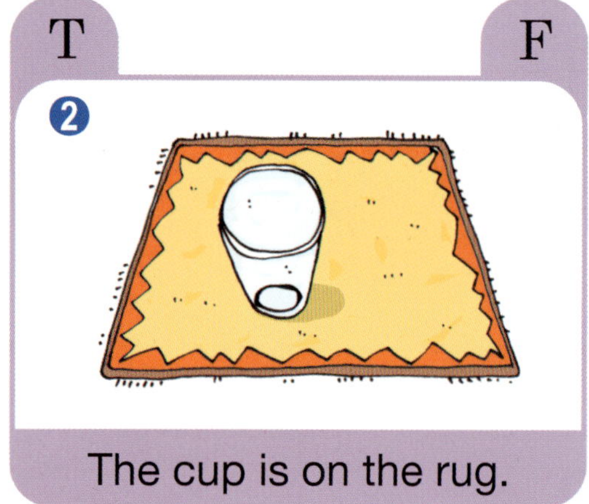

The cup is on the rug.

T   F

3

The pups hug.

T   F

4

The men cut the nut.

T   F

5

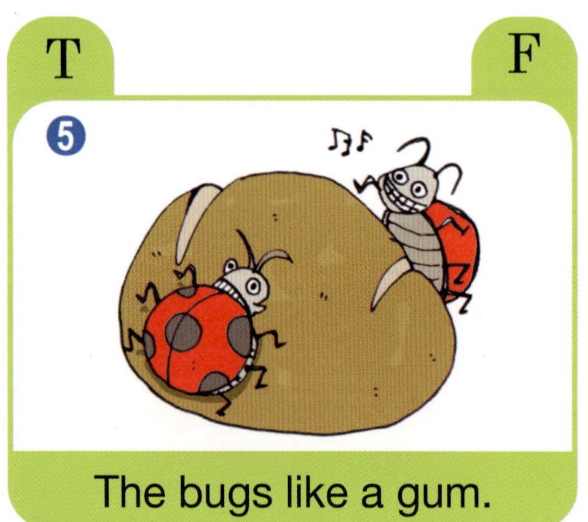

The bugs like a gum.

T   F

6

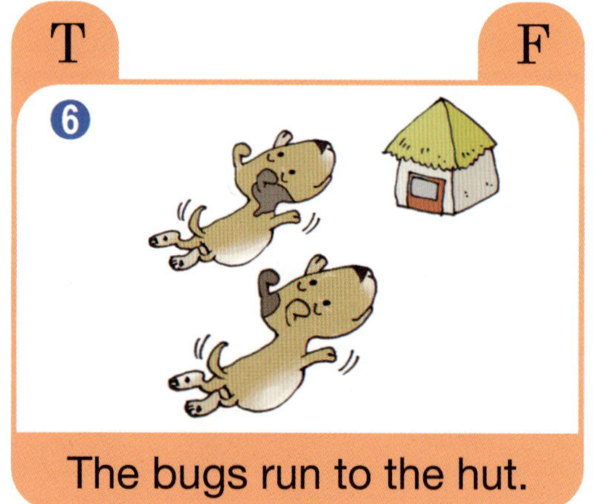

The bugs run to the hut.

Write and color.

| bug | cup | hut | pup | gum | up | hug | sun | nut |

1.

2.

3.

4.

5.

6.

7.

8.

9.

Circle the words and complete the story.

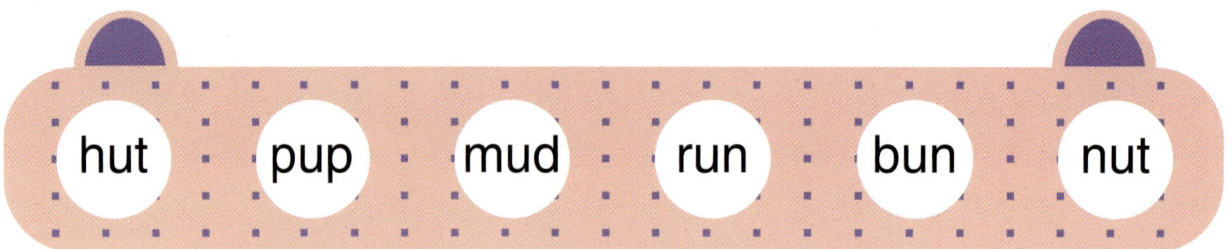

- A _______ has _______ s and _______ s.

- The _______ _______ s to the _______ .

- Oh! The _______ drops _______ s

  and _______ s in the _______ .

- What a pity!

Activity *chant*

The bug takes the gum.

The gum takes the mug.

The mug takes the gun.

The gun takes the nut.

The nut takes the top.

The top takes the pup.

The pup takes the pan.

The pan stands alone.

Look at the picture. Where are they?

1. The kid is on the (log, dog).

2. The pig is in the (box, bag).

3. The bug is on the (pin, pen).

4. The (hen, ham) is on the bed.

5. The (rat, ram) is in the pan.

6. The cat is under the (rug, leg).

7. The fox is in the (cup, cap).

Write the right letter (a, e, i, o, u).

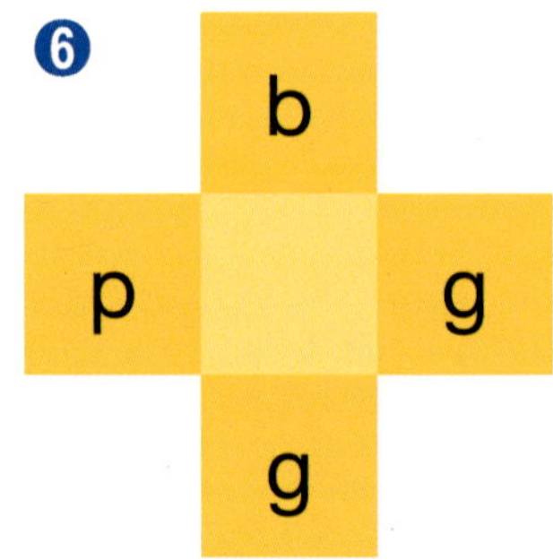

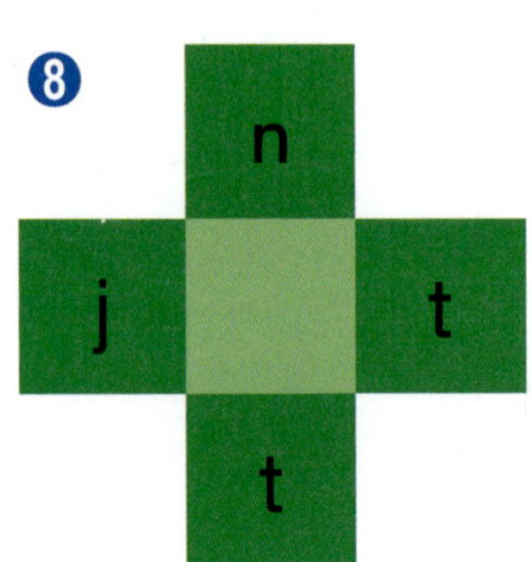

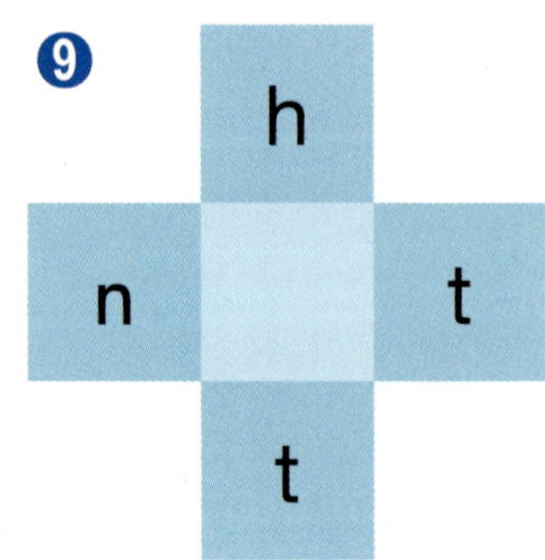

58

Listen, unscramble words and color the shapes.

[a] ★ [e] ● [i] ◆ [o] ▲ [u] ■

❶ omp ➜ mop △

❷ unb ➜

❸ asd ➜

❹ glo ➜

❺ pca ➜

❻ tis ➜

❼ mne ➜

❽ etw ➜

❾ uct ➜

❿ inf ➜

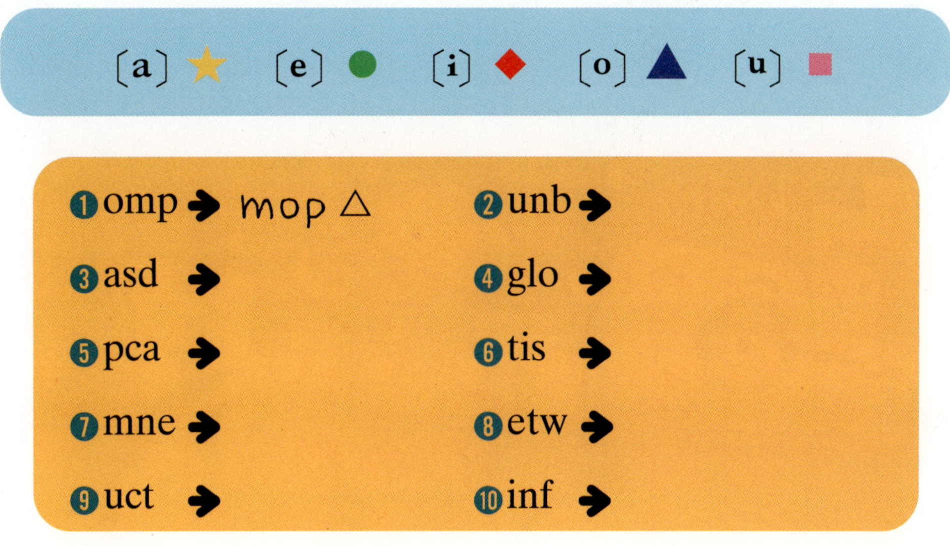

Jake likes cake and computer games.
Jake hates lace and a plane.
Jake has the same face as his twin brother.
But his brother likes a plane very much.

Who is Jake?

I am Jake.
I like cake and computer games.

I am Jake's twin brother, Dave.
I like a plane very much.

I am Jake's friend, Jane.
I like a dress with lace.

Listen, point and repeat.

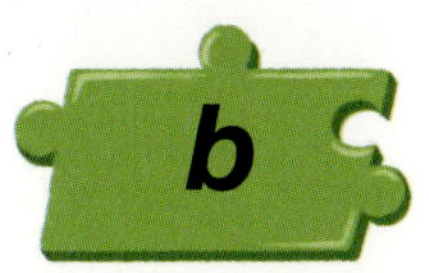 **b**	 *ake*	_______________	
 *f*	 *ace*	_______________	
 *g*	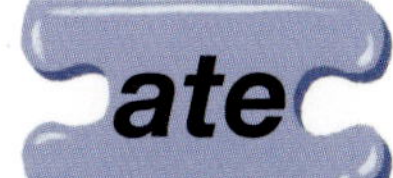 *ate*	_______________	
 *n*	 *ame*	_______________	
 *c*	 *ane*	_______________	
 *t*	 *ape*	_______________	
 *w*	 *ave*	_______________	

Listen, point and repeat.

bake

cake

lake

name

game

same

gate

hate

cave

wave

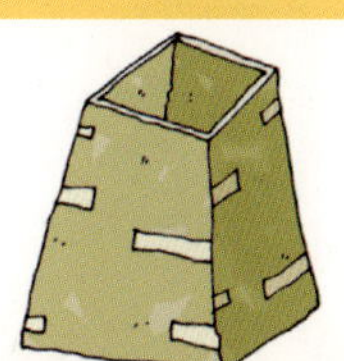

vase

case

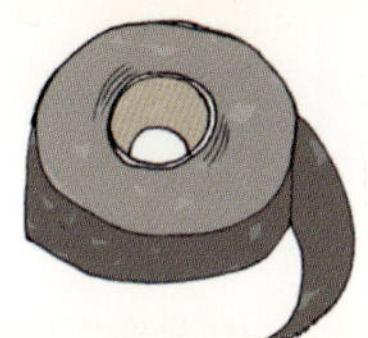

tape

cape

lace

race

face

cane

plane

mane

Sort the words according to the rhyme.

c

l

g

c

f

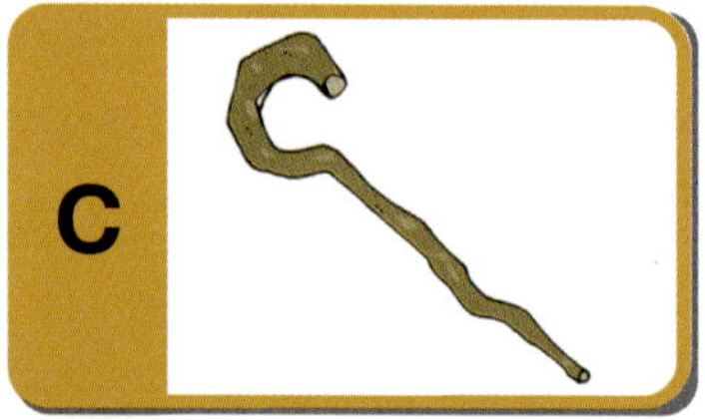
c

b

c

t

1 _ake

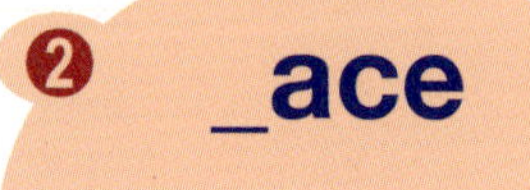
2 _ace

3 _ave

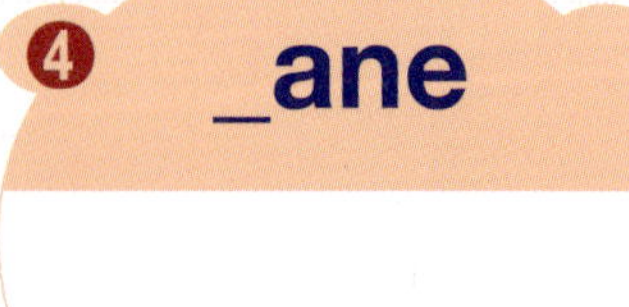
4 _ane

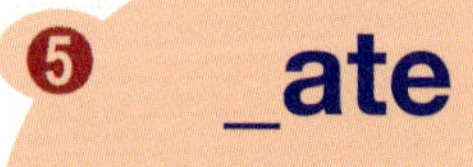
5 _ate

6 _ape

Listen and circle.

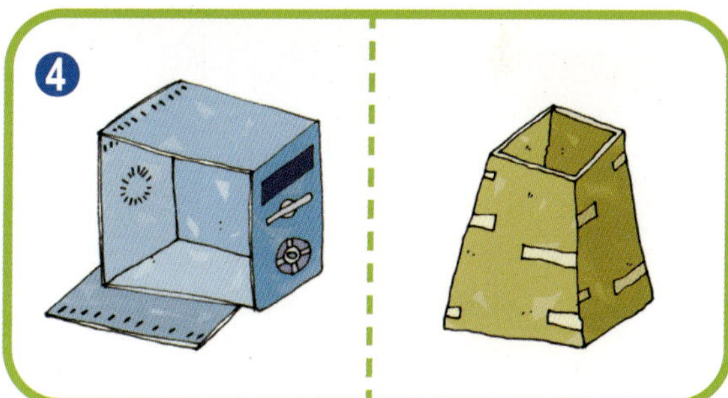

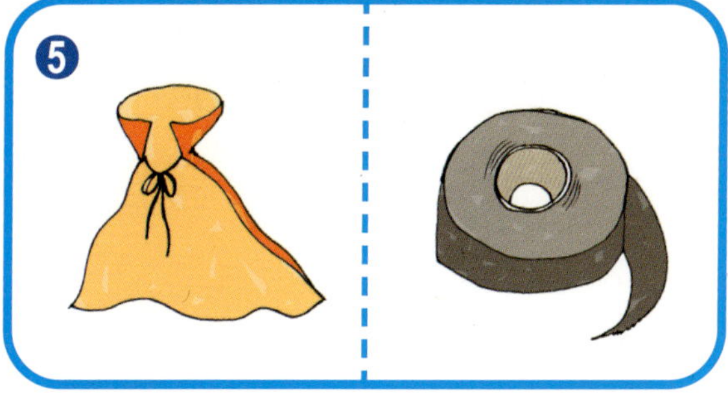

Practice – Read

Read the sentence and check the T or F.

T   F

1 

Jake bakes the cake.

T   F

2 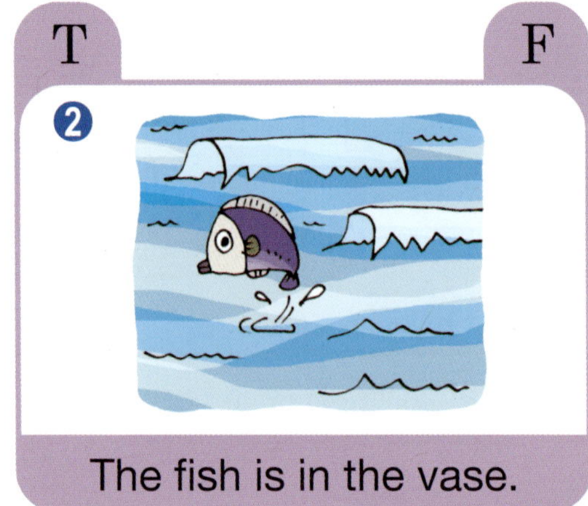

The fish is in the vase.

T   F

3 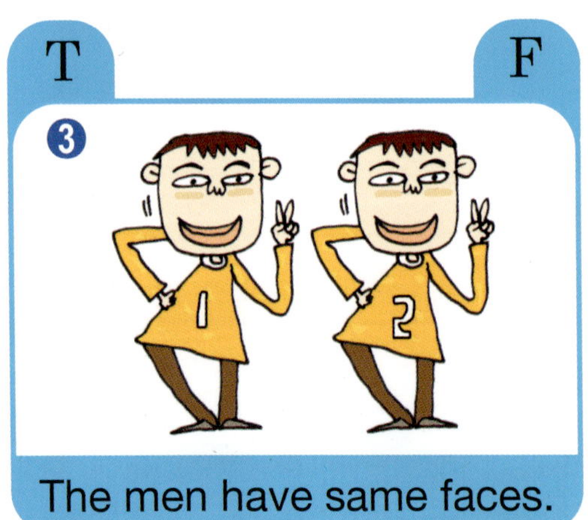

The men have same faces.

T   F

4 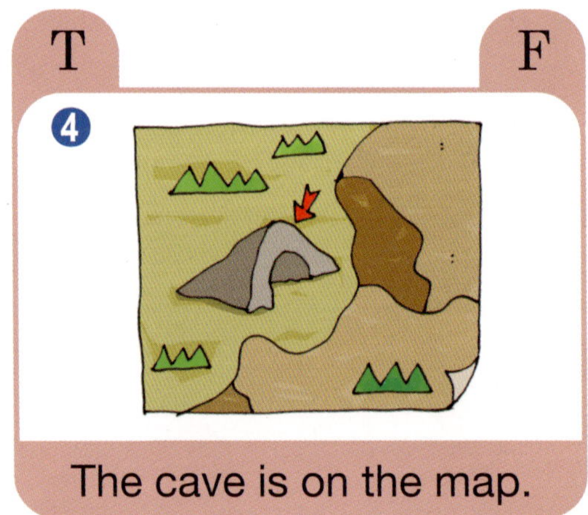

The cave is on the map.

T   F

5 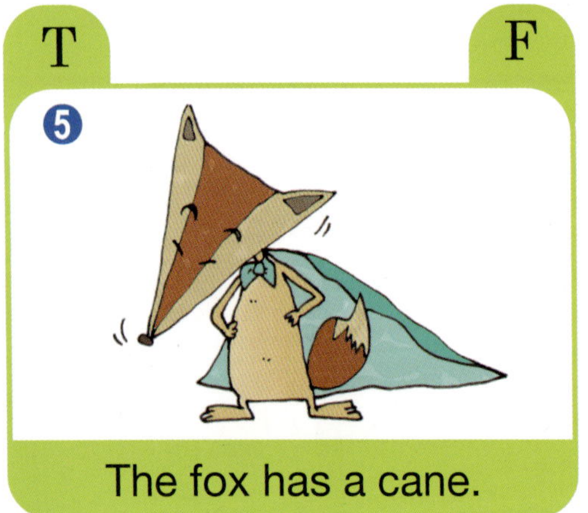

The fox has a cane.

T   F

6 

The cake is on the gate.

Write and color.

cave   race   tape   case   mane   hate   plane   game   lake

1

2

3

4

5

6

7

8

9

Circle the words and complete the story.

- Jake likes _________ and computer _________s.

- Jake _________s _________ and a _________.

- Jake has the _________ _________ as his twin brother.

- But his brother likes a _________ very much.

Open the gate, open the gate.
Say your name.
One, two, three!

Open the gate, open the gate.
Make tiny waves.
One, two, three!

Open the gate, open the gate.
Bake some cake.
For your mom!

Unit 7 Long Vowel i

I like my little brother, Mike.
I play with Mike today.
Mike hits my kite and bike.
I hide mine.
Ouch! Mike bites my leg.

Sounds

Listen and repeat.

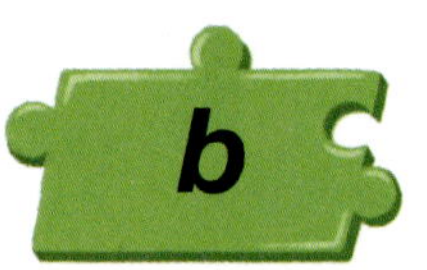
b

ike

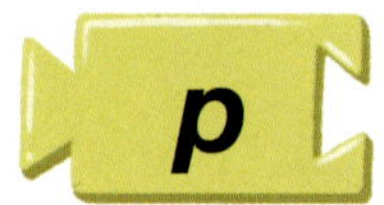
p

ine

w

ipe

r

ide

k

ite

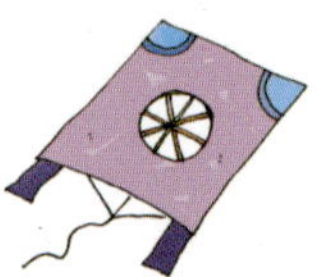

f

ive

p

ile

Listen, point and repeat.

b**i**k**e**   l**i**k**e**   h**i**k**e**

sm**i**l**e**   w**i**p**e**   p**i**l**e**

b**i**t**e**   k**i**t**e**   s**i**d**e**

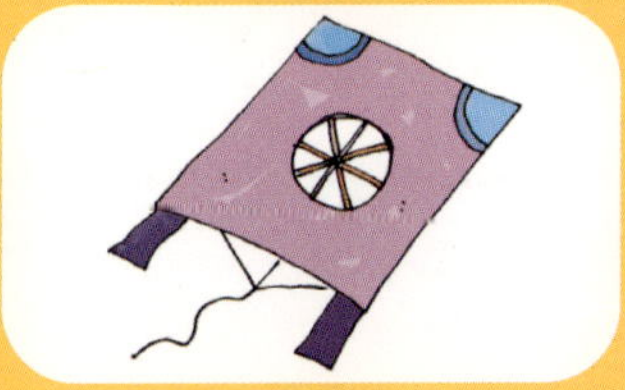

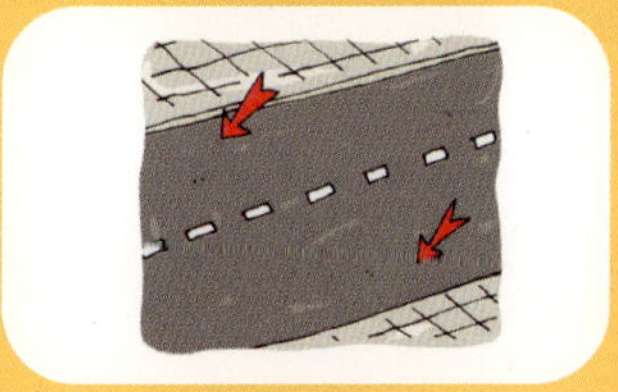

r**i**d**e**   d**i**v**e**   f**i**v**e**

p**i**n**e**   l**i**n**e**

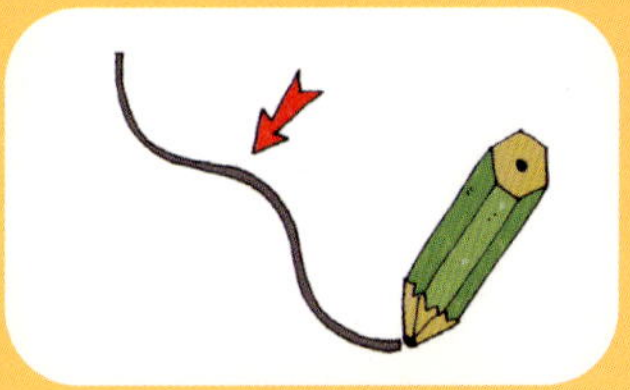

Sort the words according to the rhyme.

h

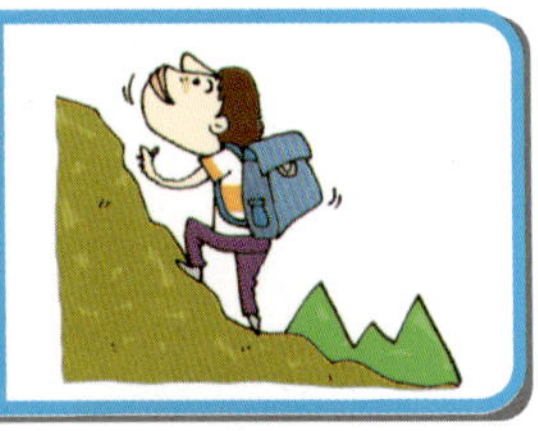

s

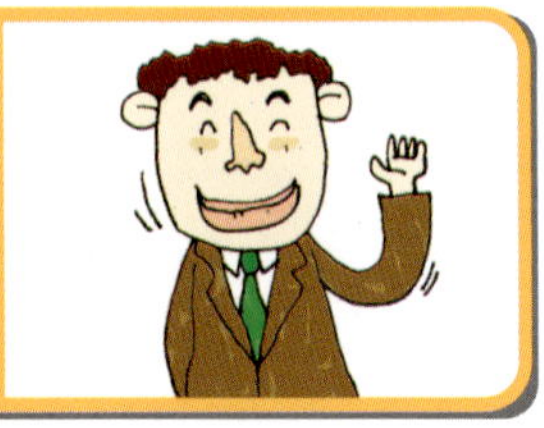

f

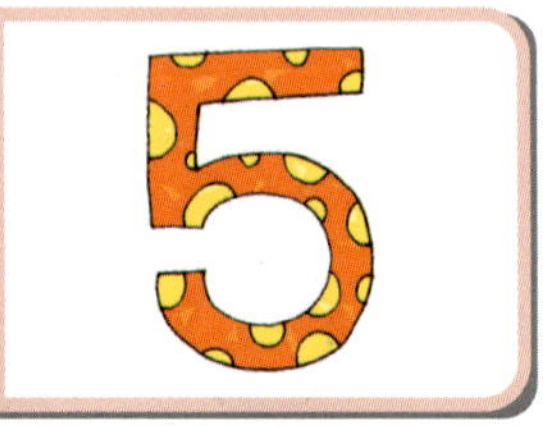

b

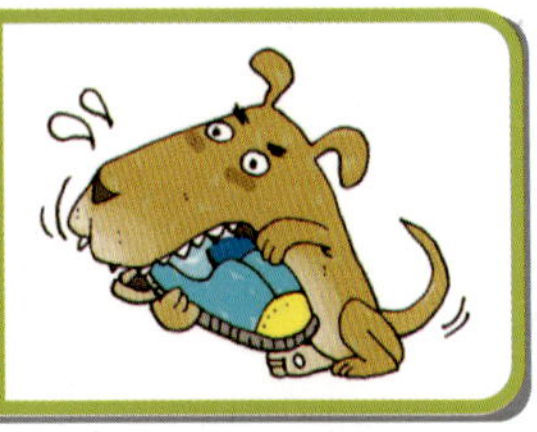

r

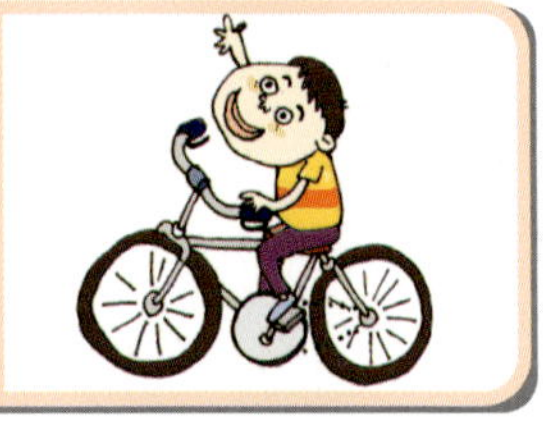

k

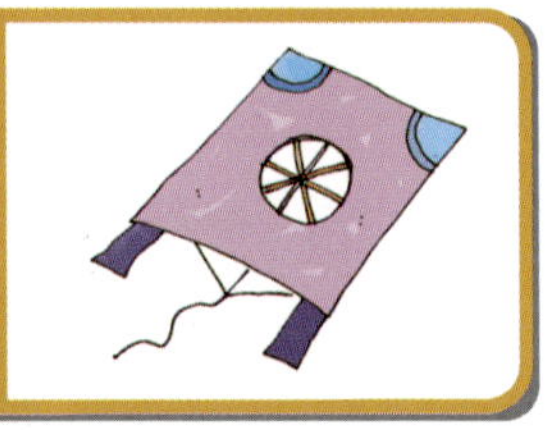

s

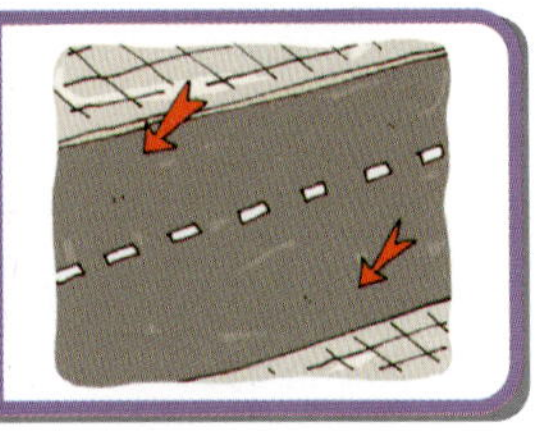

p

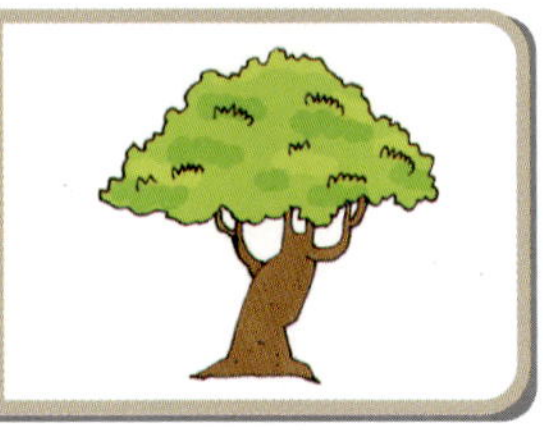

b

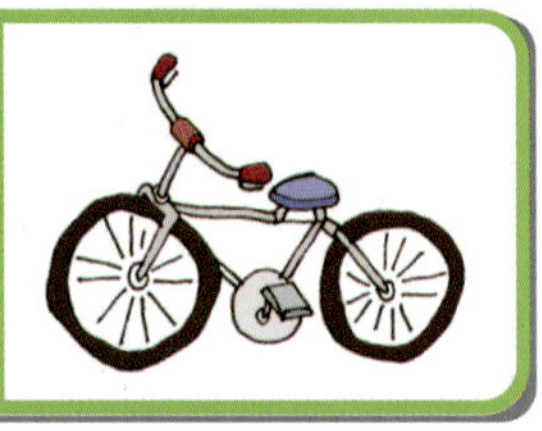

① _ike

② _ide

③ _ile

④ _ine

⑤ _ite

⑥ _ive

Listen and circle.

Read the sentence and check the T or F.

T   F

1 

The kid rides a bike.

T   F

2 

The kid is flying a kite.

T   F

3 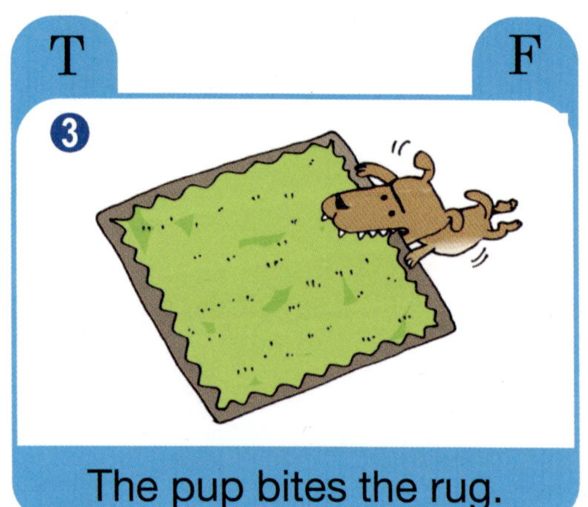

The pup bites the rug.

T   F

4 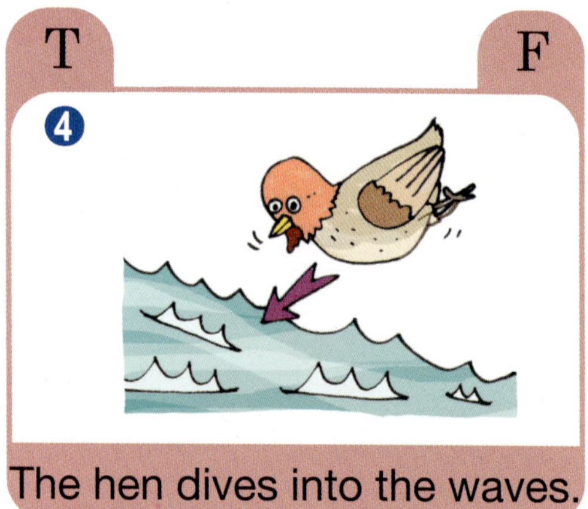

The hen dives into the waves.

T   F

5 

The dog likes the cake.

T   F

6 

The man wipes the bike.

Write and color.

pine   bike   five   smile   hike   ride   bite   dive   kite

1

2

3

4

5

6

7

8

9

Circle the words and complete the story.

- I _______ my little brother Mike.

- I play with Mike today.

- Mike hits my _______ and _______.

- I hide mine.

- Ouch! Mike _______s my leg.

Two kids are lined up
side by side, side by side.

The kids ride the bikes
side by side, side by side.

The kites fly in the sky
side by side, side by side.

The kids wave to the pine tree
side by side, side by side.

Unit 8 Long Vowel O

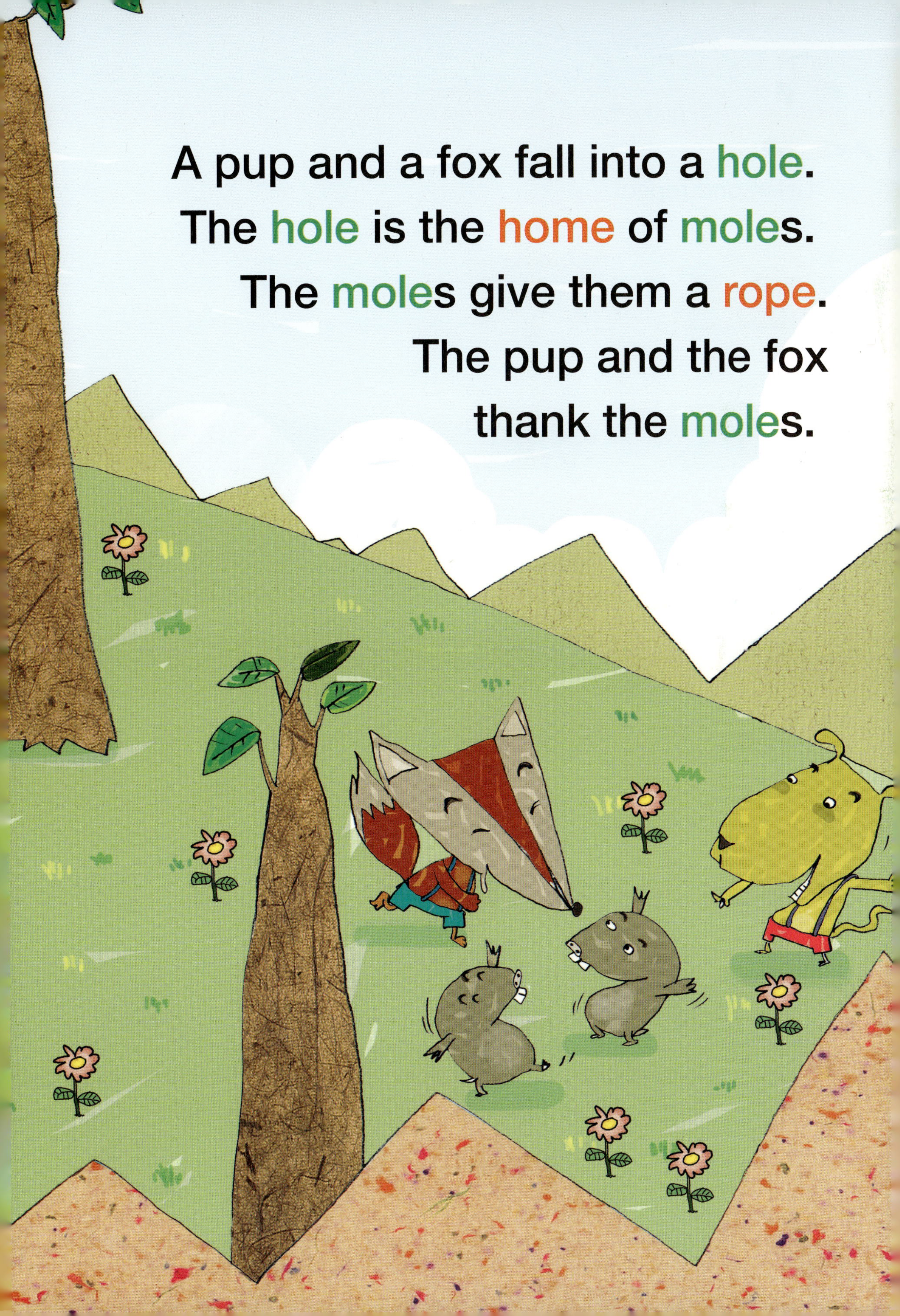
A pup and a fox fall into a hole.
The hole is the home of moles.
The moles give them a rope.
The pup and the fox
thank the moles.

Listen and repeat.

 n  ose 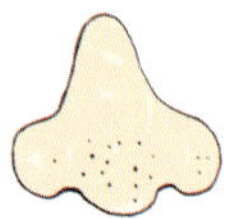

 n 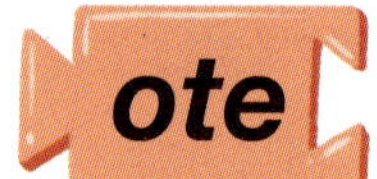 ote 

 c  one 

 h  ole 

 h  ose 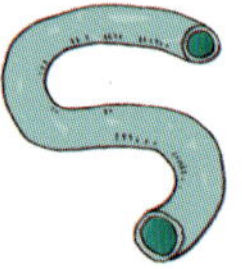

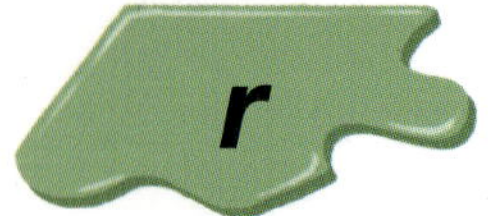 r  obe 

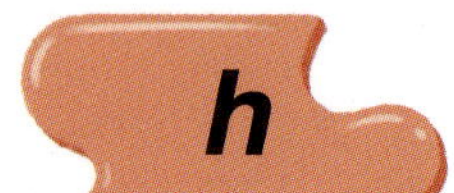 h  ome 

Listen, point and repeat.

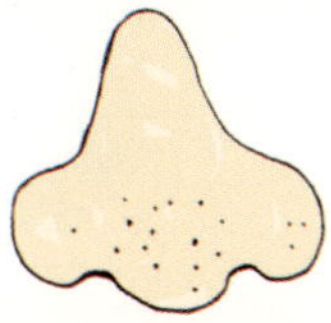

nose	 rose	 rope
 hope	 vote	 note
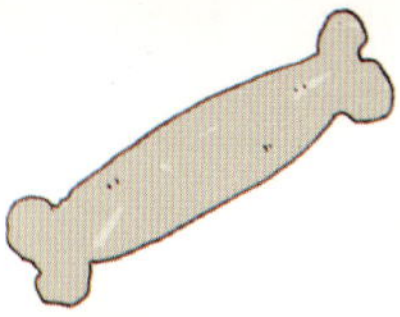 bone	 cone	 pole
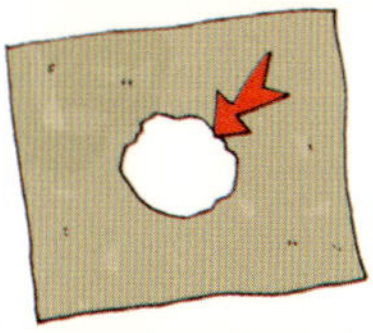 hole	 mole	 home
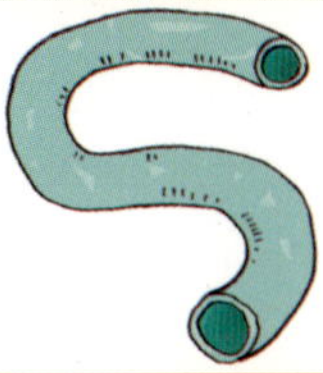 hose	 robe	

Practice

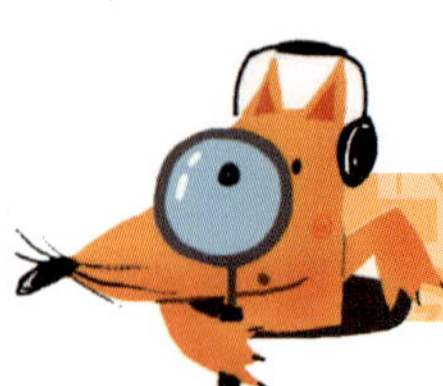

Sort the words according to the rhyme.

r 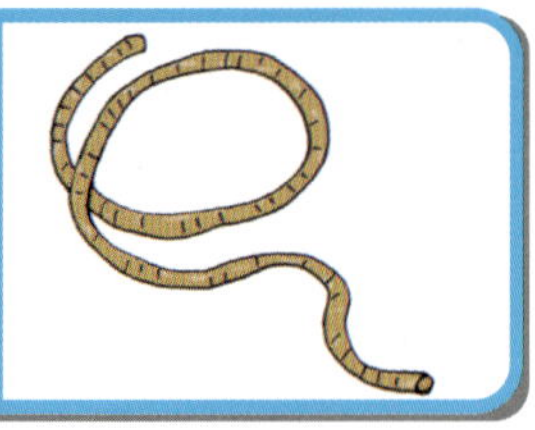

h 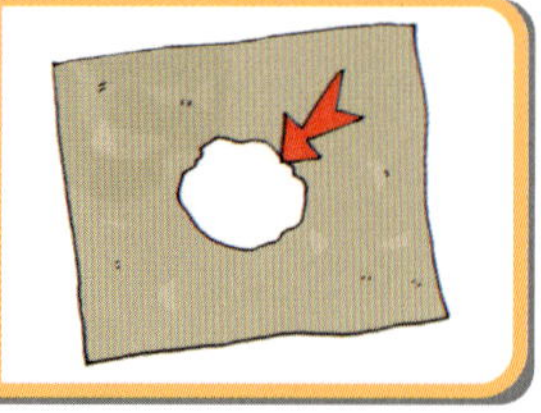

c 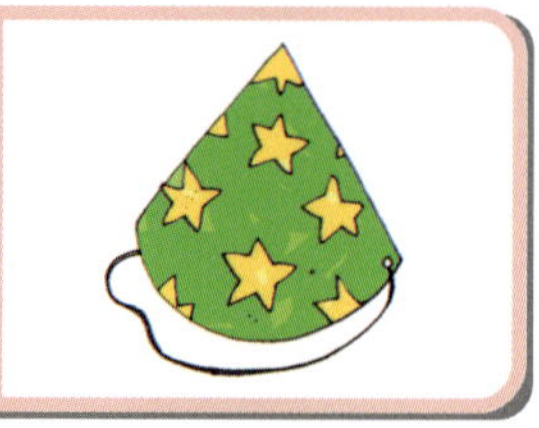

m 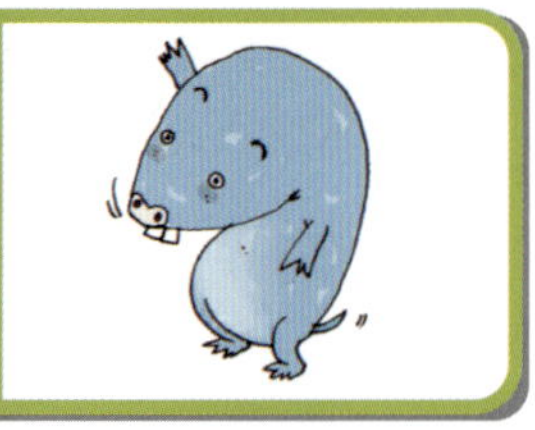

n 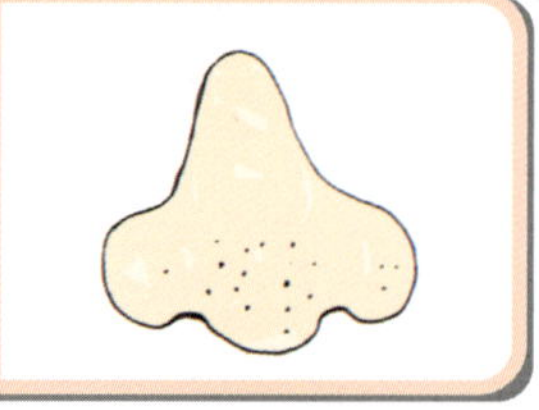

n 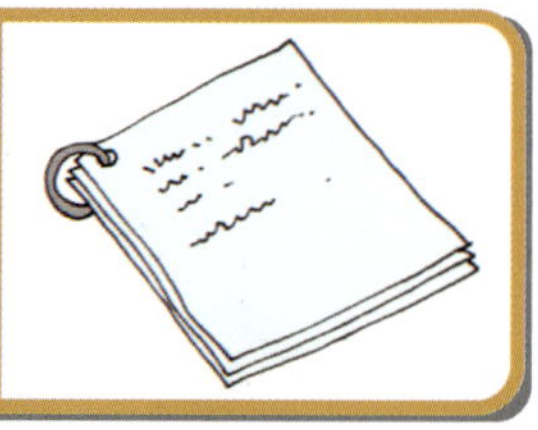

b 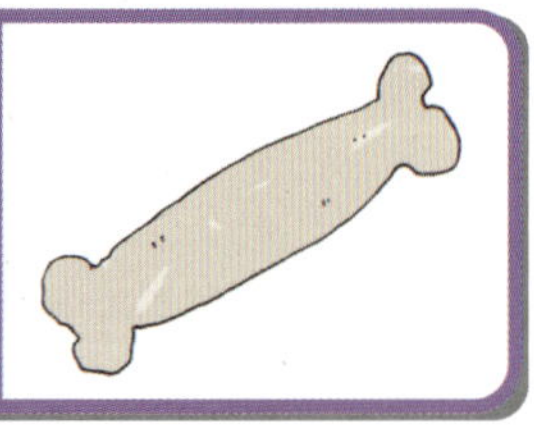

v 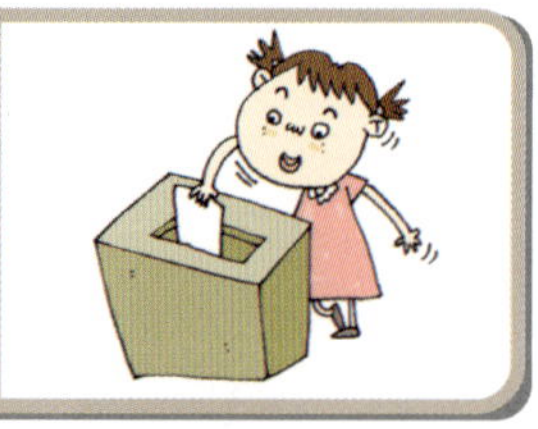

r 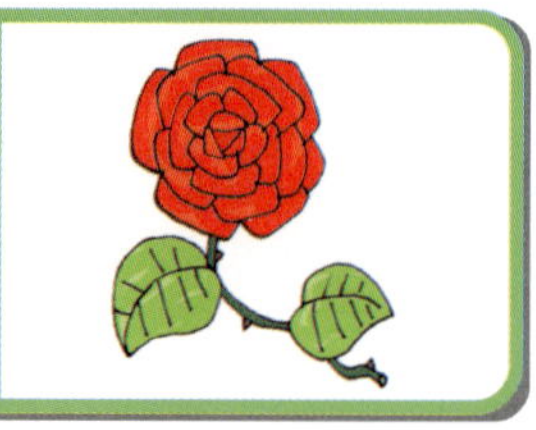

1. _ole

2. _one

3. _ope

4. _ose

5. _ote

Listen and circle.

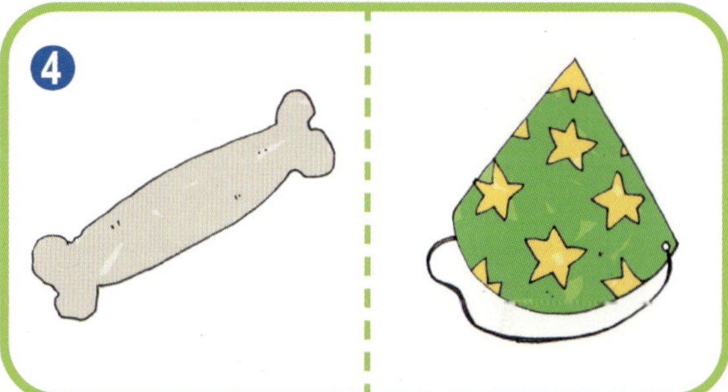

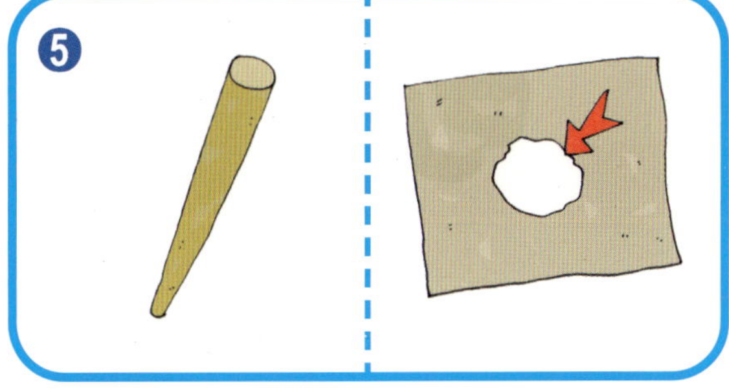

Read the sentence and check the T or F.

T   F

1

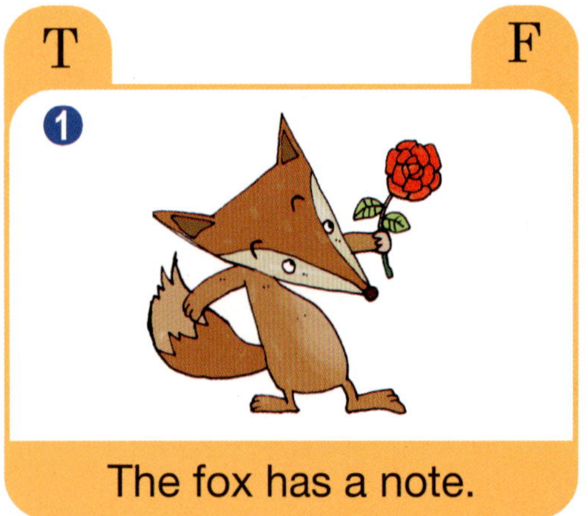

The fox has a note.

T   F

2

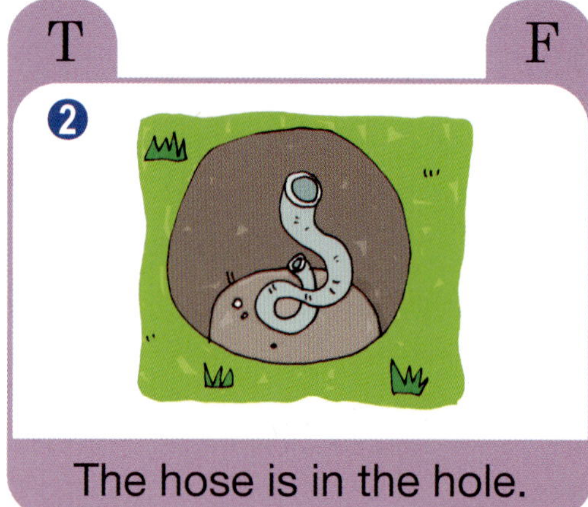

The hose is in the hole.

T   F

3

The pup has a bone.

T   F

4

The kite is on the pole.

T   F

5

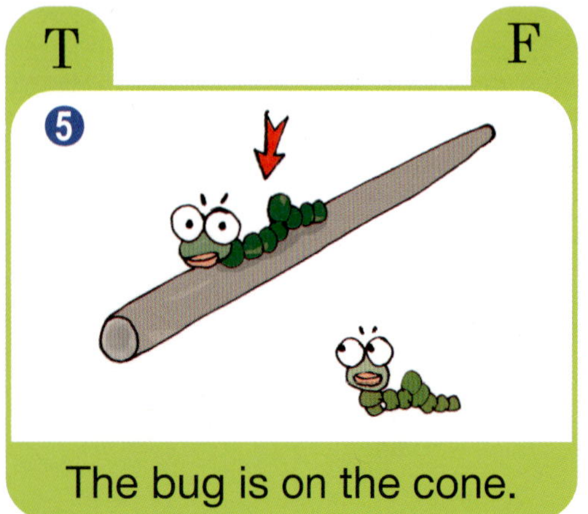

The bug is on the cone.

T   F

6

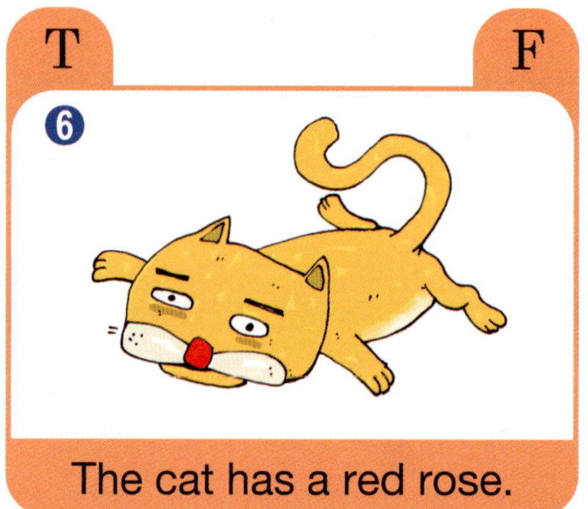

The cat has a red rose.

Write and color.

rope   rose   hose   cone   home   bone   mole   vote   hope

1

2

3

4

5

6

7

8

9

Circle the words and complete the story.

- A pup and a fox fall into a  __________.

- The [image] __________ is the home of [image] __________s.

- The [image] __________s give them a [image] __________.

- The pup and the fox thank the [image] __________s.

Activity *chant*

Let's play hide and seek!
Let's hide away!
One, two, three, four, five!

The mole is in the hole.
The bug is on the pole.
The cat is hanging on the rope.
The rat is in the hose.

Unit 9 Long Vowel u

A cute kid is on the mule
in the sand dunes.
The kid is very hot and thirsty.
But, there is no water in his bottle.
His hope is to get a huge ice cube.

Listen and repeat.

 c  ube 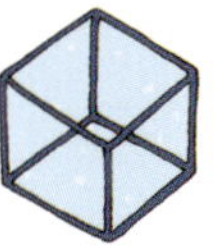

 t  une 

 m  ule 

 c  ute 

 h  uge 

 d  uke 

 r  ude 

Listen, point and repeat.

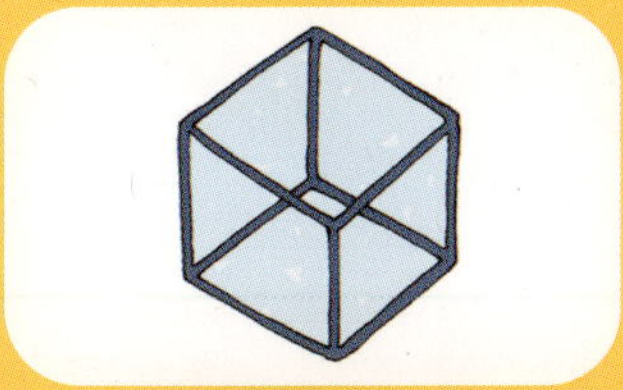

cube	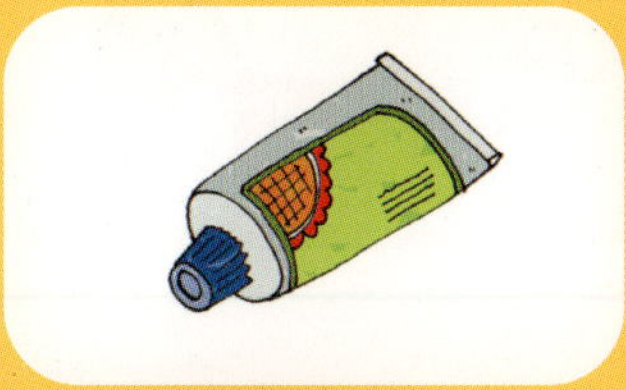 tube	June
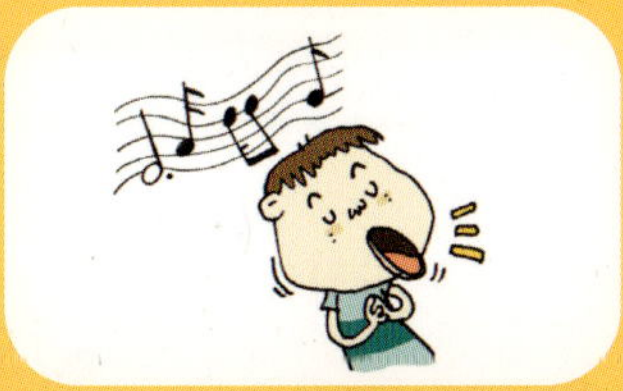 tune	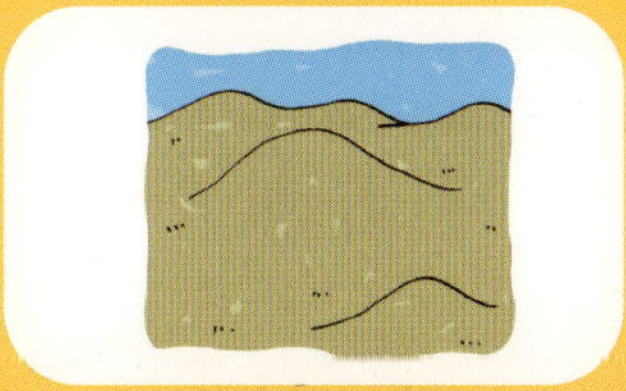 dune	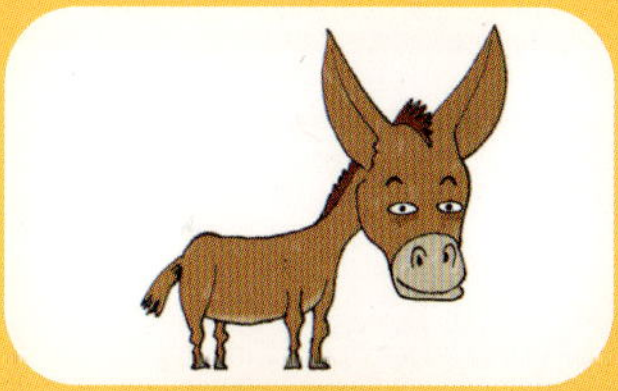 mule
fuse	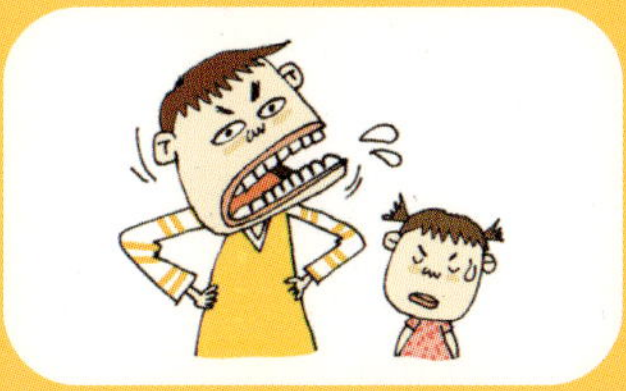 rude	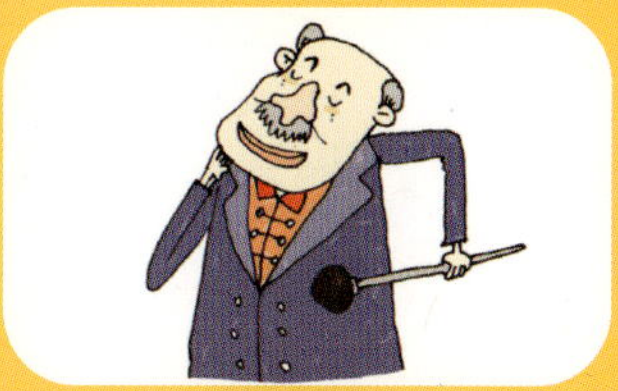 duke
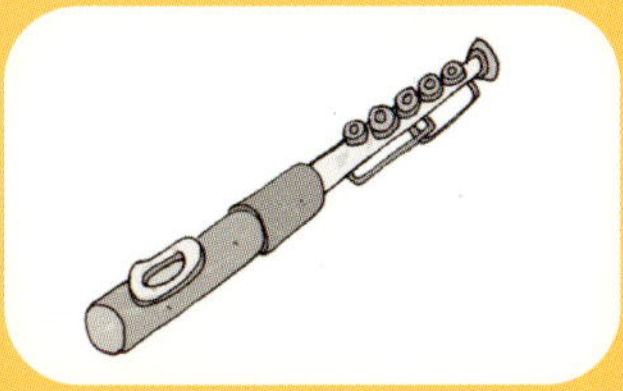 flute	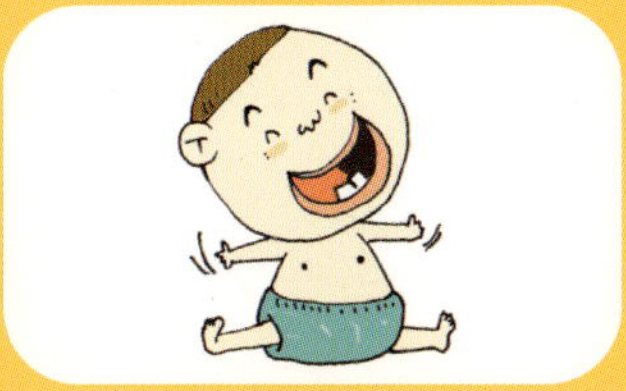 cute	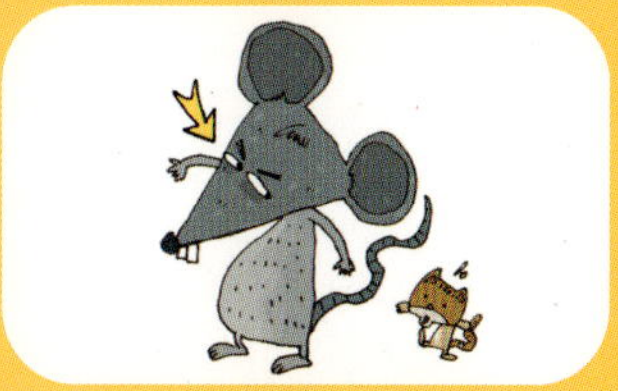 huge

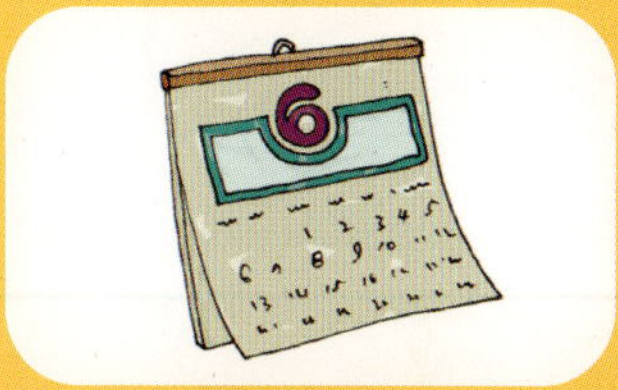

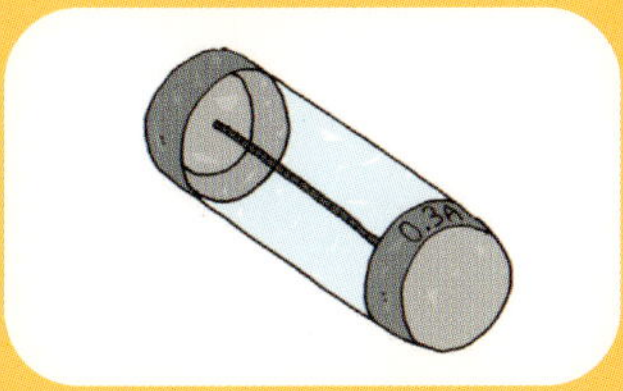

Sort the words according to the rhyme.

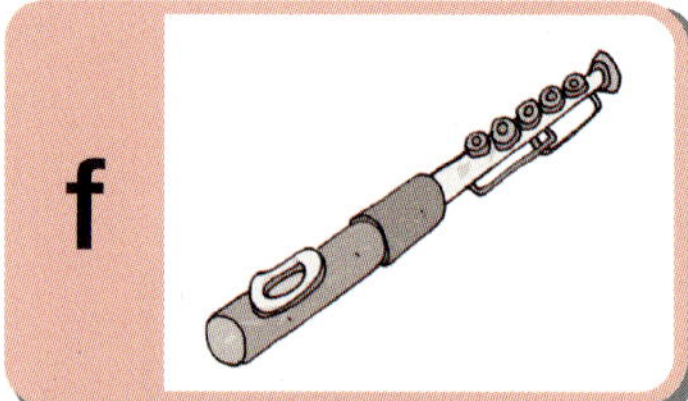

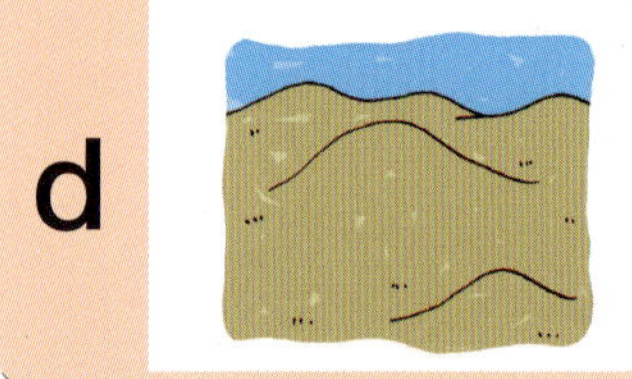

Listen and circle.

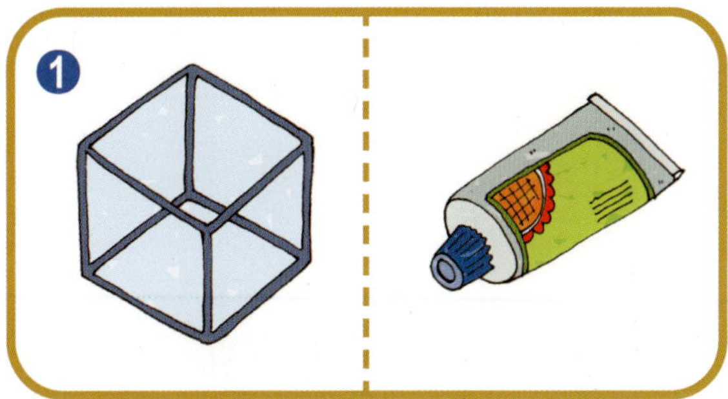

Read the sentence and check the T or F.

1 T ___ F ___

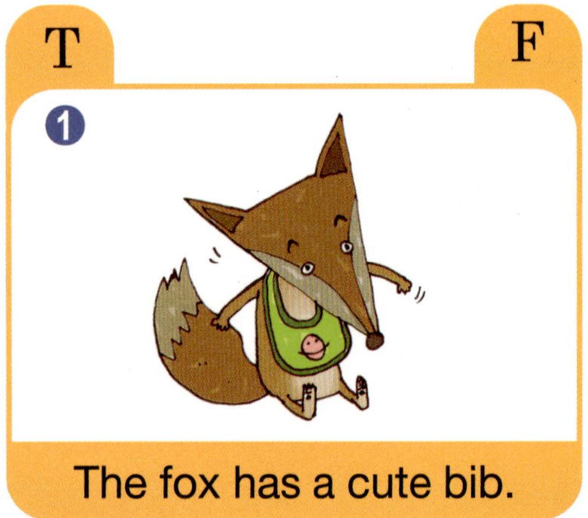

The fox has a cute bib.

2 T ___ F ___

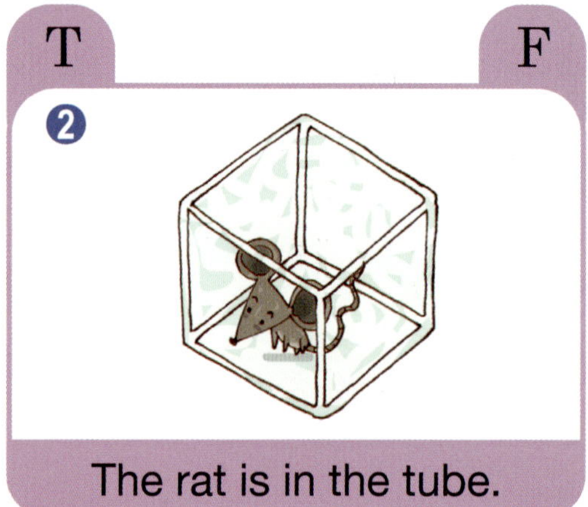

The rat is in the tube.

3 T ___ F ___

The duke is very rude.

4 T ___ F ___

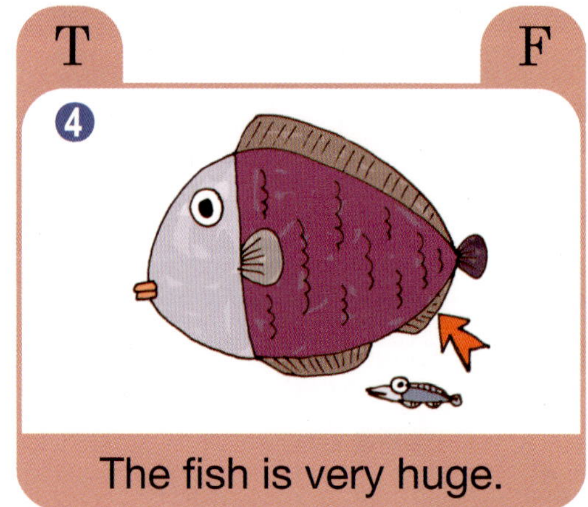

The fish is very huge.

5 T ___ F ___

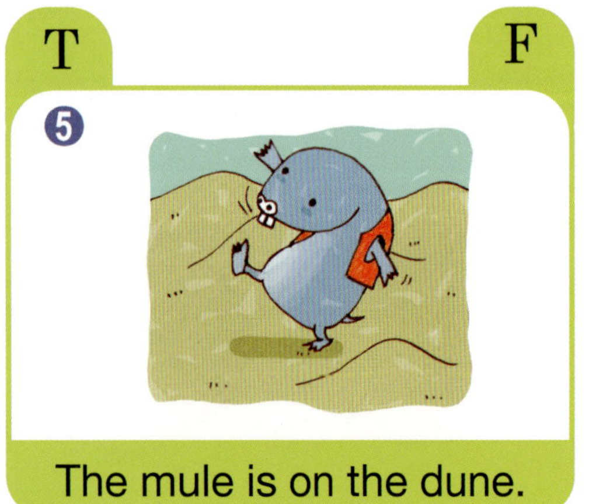

The mule is on the dune.

6 T ___ F ___

The mule has a flute.

Write and color.

flute   huge   June   cube   rude   cute   tune   tube   duke

Circle the words and complete the story.

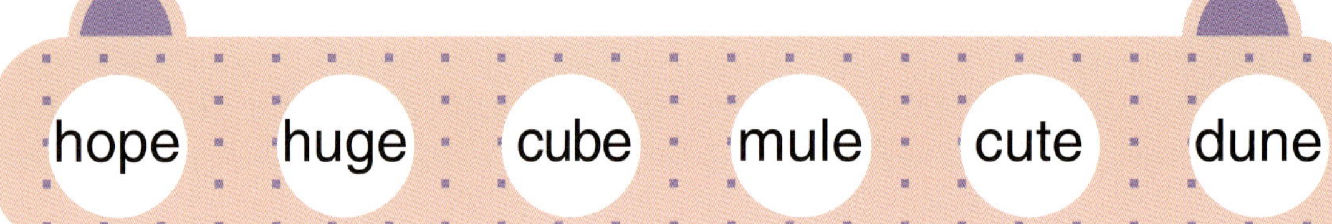

- A _________ kid is on the _________ in the sand _________ s.

- The kid is very hot and thirsty.

- But, there is no water in his bottle.

- His hope is to get a _________ ice _________ .

Activity *chant*

What's in the cube?
A case in the cube.
A case in the cube.

What's in the case?
A flute in the case.
A flute in the case.

What's in the tube?
A train in the tube.
A train in the tube.

What's in the train?
A cute baby in the train.
A cute baby in the train.

Review 2

Name each picture and circle the word you hear.

Write the right letter.

Color the picture with long vowel a green, the picture with long vowel i pink, the picture with long vowel o yellow.

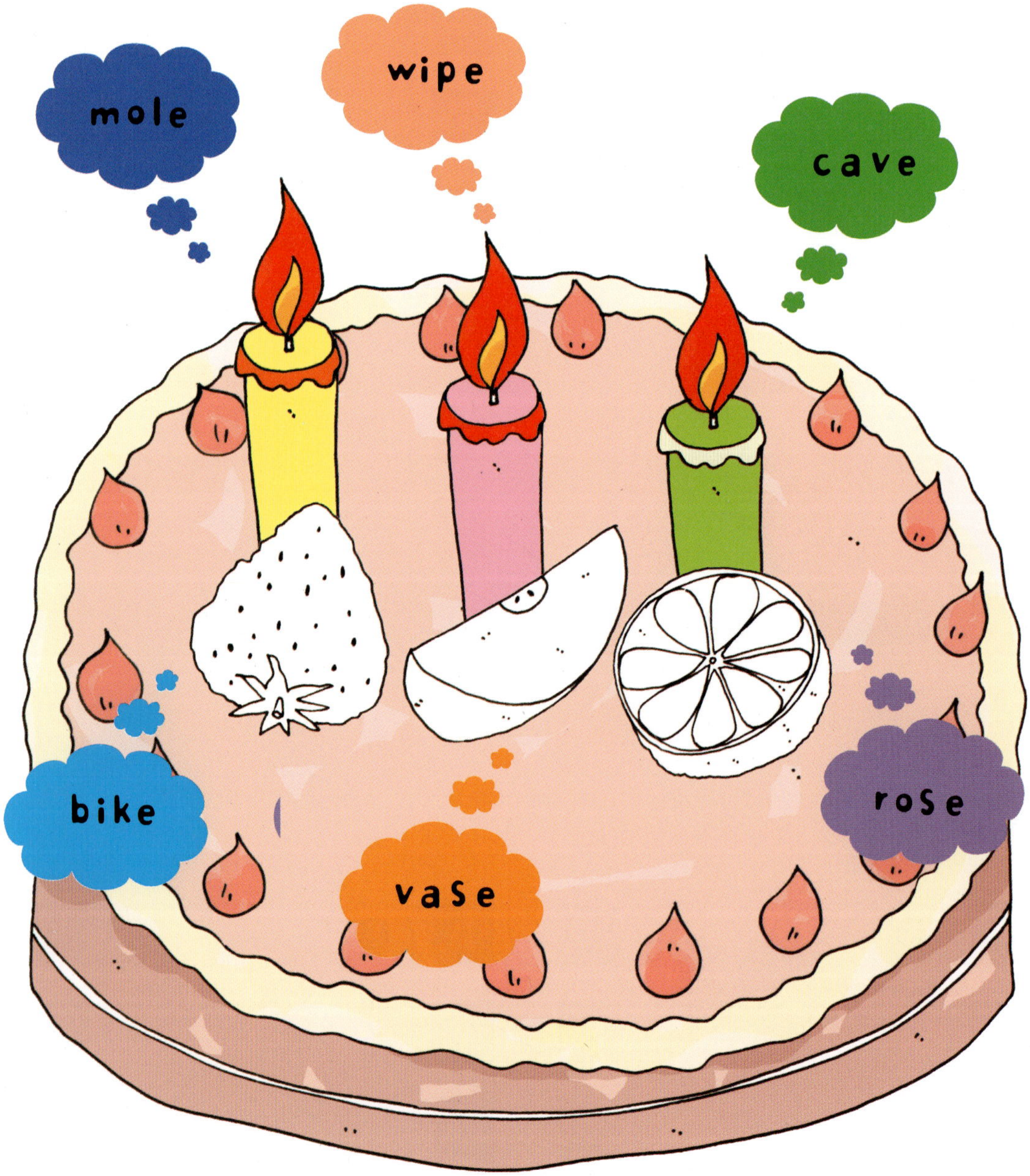

Listen and circle the word with the long a, i, o, u in each sentence. Write it on the line.

1 

The kids have same faces.

same   face

2 

The red fox hikes mountain.

3 

The mole is in the hole.

4 

The dog bites the kid's leg.

5 

The red hen is on the gate.

6 

The dog hates the cat.

Test

Listen and circle.

 1    ⓐ rat   ⓑ red   ⓒ rug ✓

2    ⓐ lap   ⓑ lip   ⓒ pup

3    ⓐ hen   ⓑ fin   ⓒ bun

4    ⓐ net   ⓑ nut   ⓒ hot

5    ⓐ pan   ⓑ pen   ⓒ bun

6    ⓐ case   ⓑ cube   ⓒ cute

Find and circle the words.

1. fenietopie**aten**eit

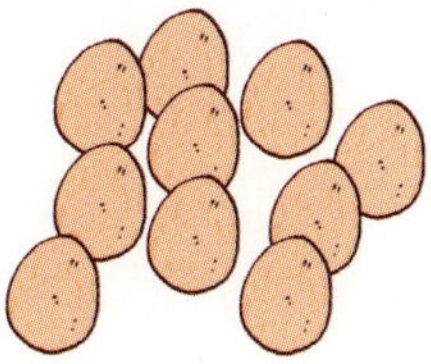

2. poinmaninamopiet

3. leiputoalepileenuda

4. duaketoneconecipt

5. dacakedukebaone

6. lacipolipilatepune

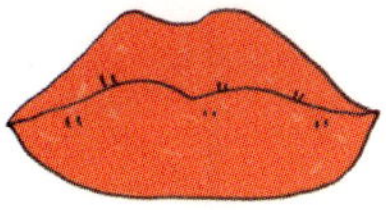

Test

Listen and check.

1

2
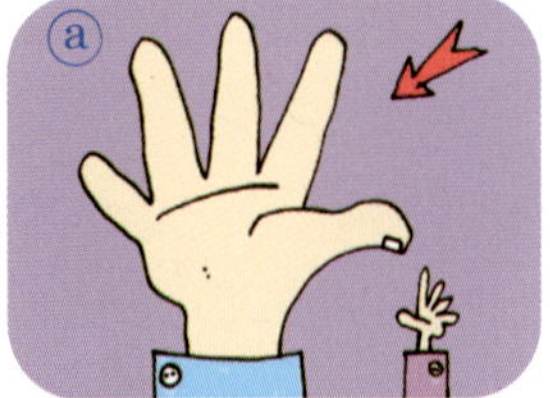

3

4
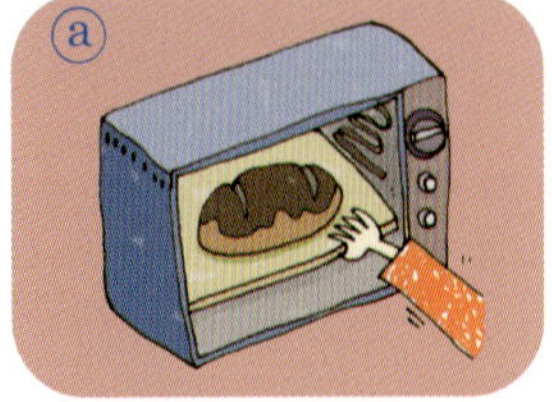

5

6
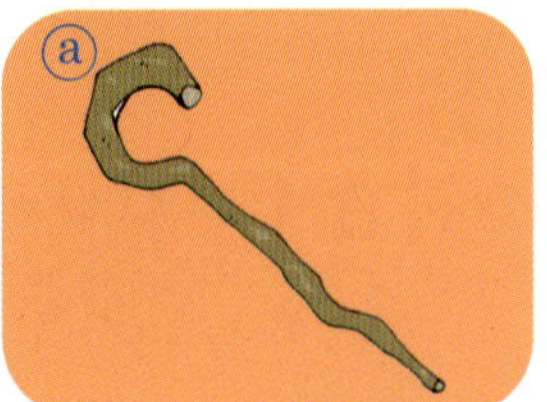

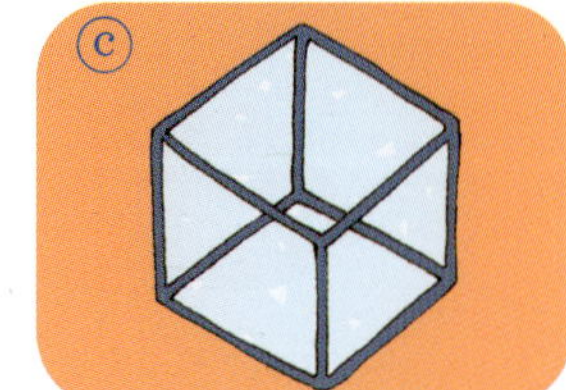

7 -ase

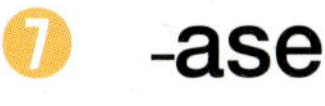 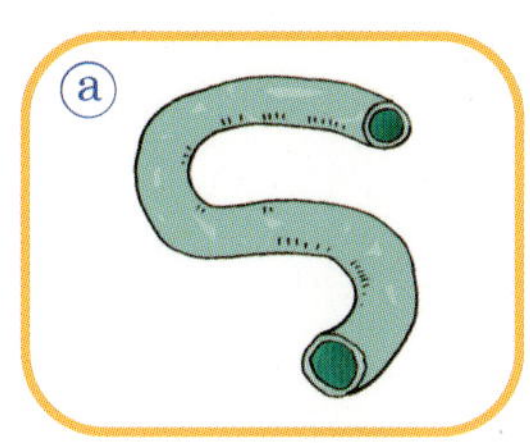  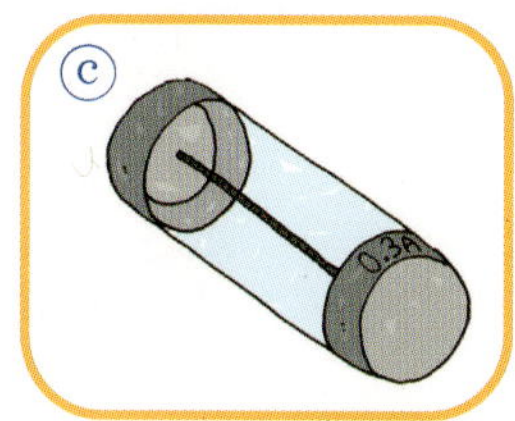

8 -ude

9 -ole

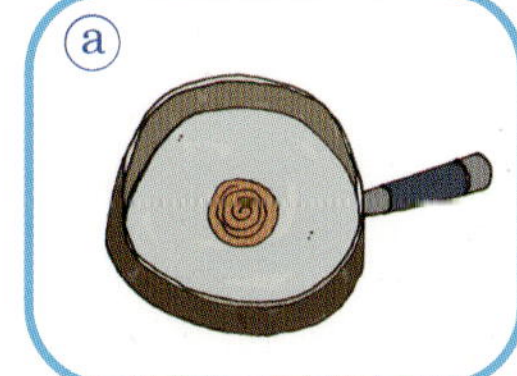  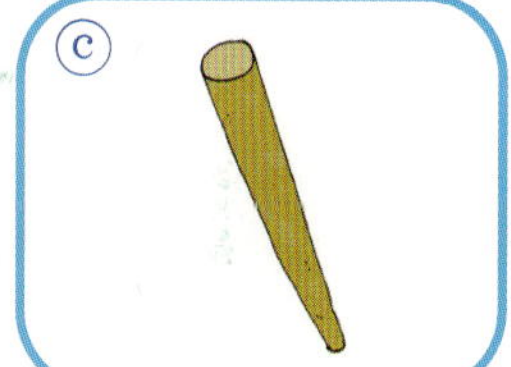

10 -ug

11 -am

  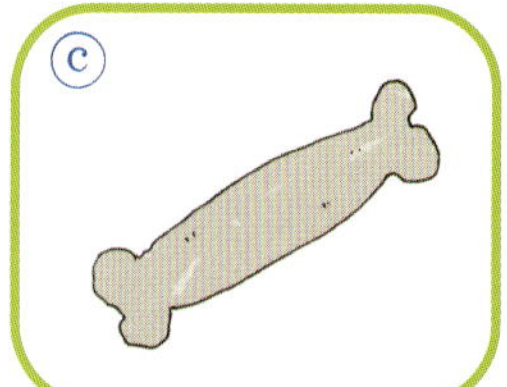

12 -ot

  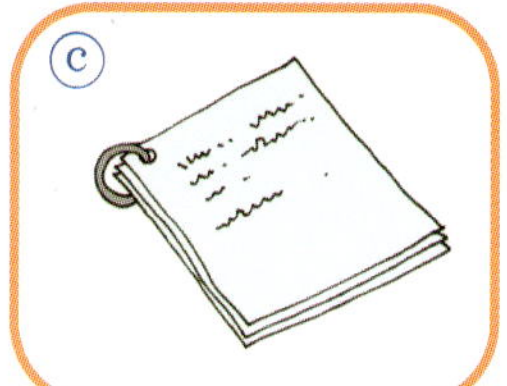

Test

Unscramble each word.

1. anv

van

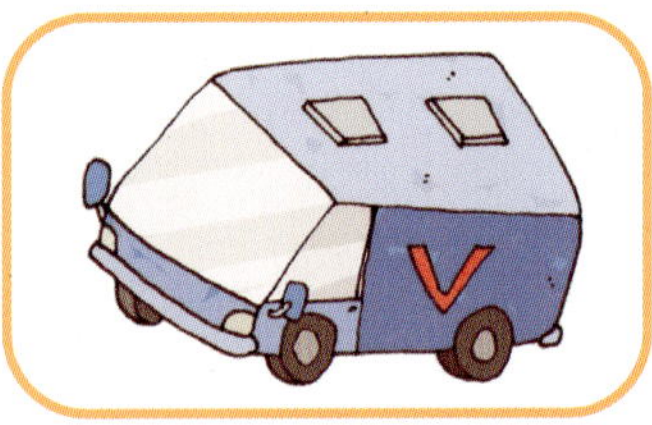

2. tulfe

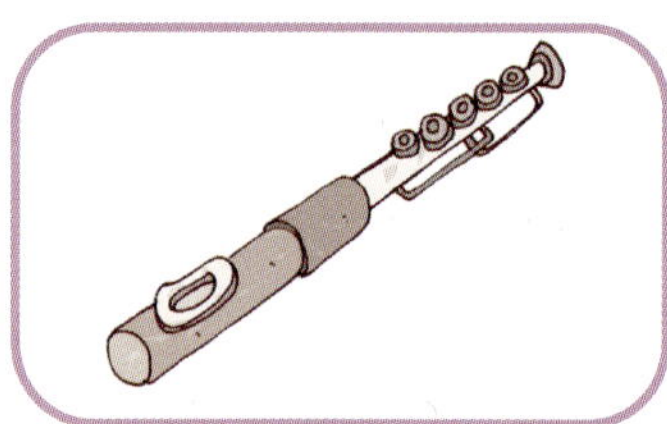

3. ilek

4. cale

5. poeh

6. uns

Listen and write.

1. The fox is hopping with a _pot_ .

2. The red ______ is ______.

3. Jake has a ______ and a ______.

4. The kid likes a ______ ______.

5. The ______ runs to the ______.

6. The pig and the dog fall into a ______.

Answer Key

10p

1 ram
  jam
2 fat
  mat
3 cap
  lap
4 pan
  man
5 bad

11p

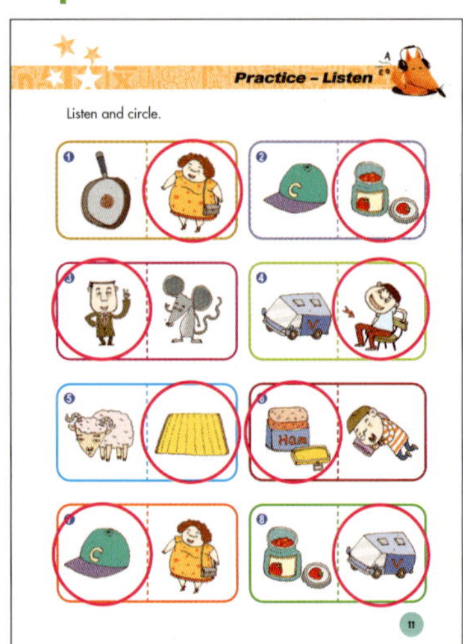

12p

2 F
3 F
4 F
5 F
6 T

13p

2 van
3 nap
4 mat
5 pan
6 ham
7 rat
8 cap
9 jam

14p

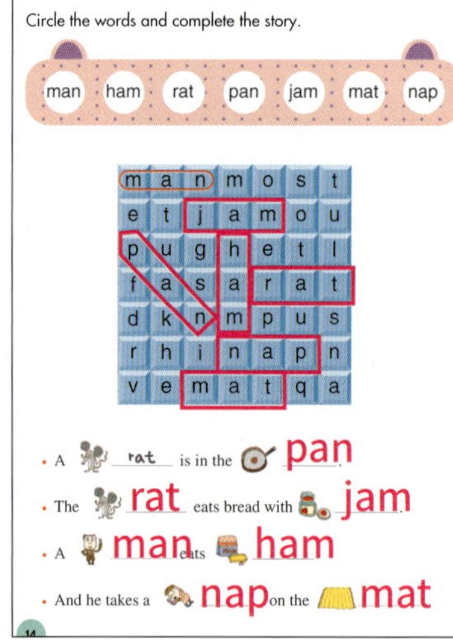

20p

1 red
  wed
  bed
2 egg
  leg
3 hen
  pen
4 net
  jet

21p

22p

1 F
2 T
3 F
4 T
5 T
6 T

23p

1 leg
2 ten
3 egg
4 bed
5 pen
6 jet
7 hen
8 net
9 red

24p

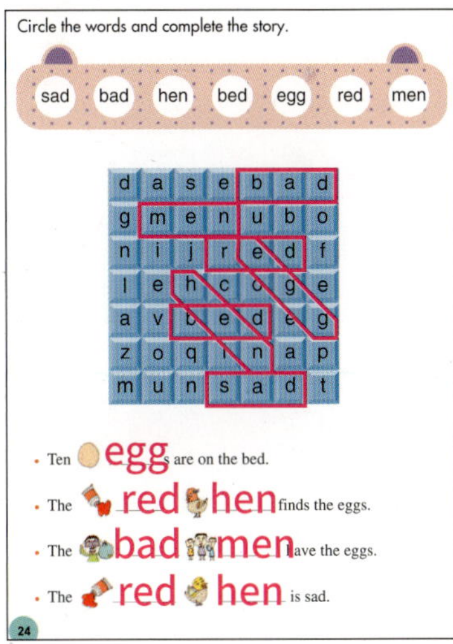

31p

34p

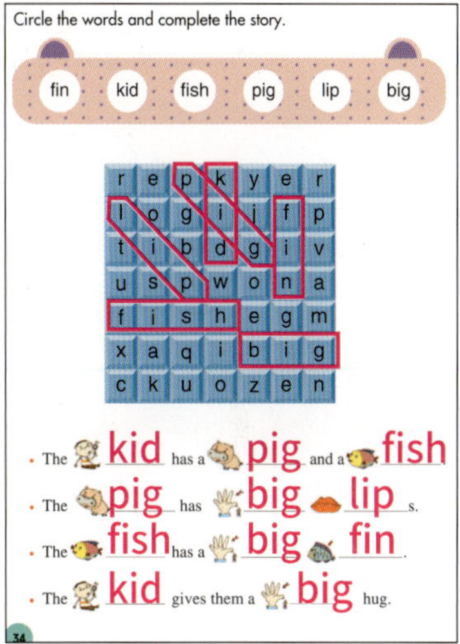

30p

❶ kid

❷ pig

  big

❸ pin

  fin

❹ sit

  hit

❺ lip

❻ six

32p

❶ F

❷ F

❸ T

❹ T

❺ T

❻ T

33p

❶ fish

❷ six

❸ bib

❹ lip

❺ kid

❻ big

❼ pig

❽ sit

❾ lid

40p

❶ dog

  log

❷ mop

  hop

  top

❸ pot

  hot

❹ fox

  box

Answer Key

41p

44p

51p

42p

❶ T
❷ F
❸ F
❹ T
❺ T
❻ F

43p

❶ top
❷ fox
❸ box
❹ log
❺ jog
❻ dog
❼ pot
❽ hot
❾ nod

50p

❶ rug
   bug
❷ bun
   sun
❸ pup
   cup
   up
❹ hut
   cut

52p

❶ T
❷ T
❸ T
❹ F
❺ F
❻ F

53p

❶ pup
❷ cup
❸ gum
❹ bug
❺ up
❻ sun
❼ hut
❽ hug
❾ nut

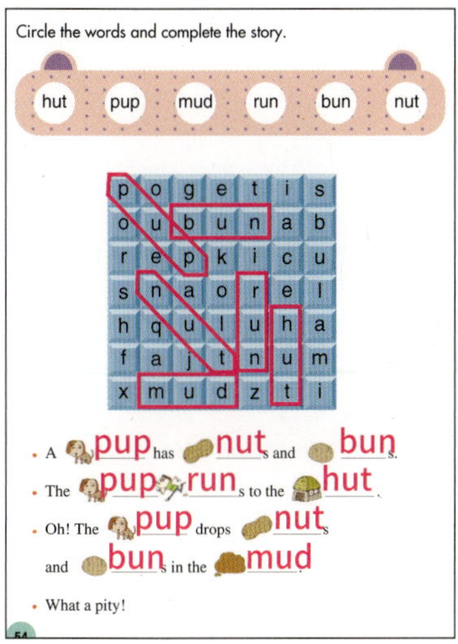

Review1

57p

❶ log   ❷ box
❸ pin   ❹ hen
❺ rat   ❻ rug
❼ cup

58p

❶ u   ❷ o   ❸ i
❹ a   ❺ e   ❻ i
❼ a   ❽ e   ❾ u

59p

❶ mop ▲   ❷ bun ■
❸ sad ★   ❹ log ▲
❺ cap ★   ❻ sit ◆
❼ men ●   ❽ wet ●
❾ cut ■   ❿ fin ◆

66p

❶ cake
  bake
❷ lace
  face
❸ cave
❹ cane
❺ gate
❻ tape
  cape

67p

68p

❶ T
❷ F
❸ T
❹ T
❺ F
❻ F

Answer Key

69p

❶ tape
❷ hate
❸ game
❹ race
❺ lake
❻ case
❼ plane
❽ cave
❾ mane

70p

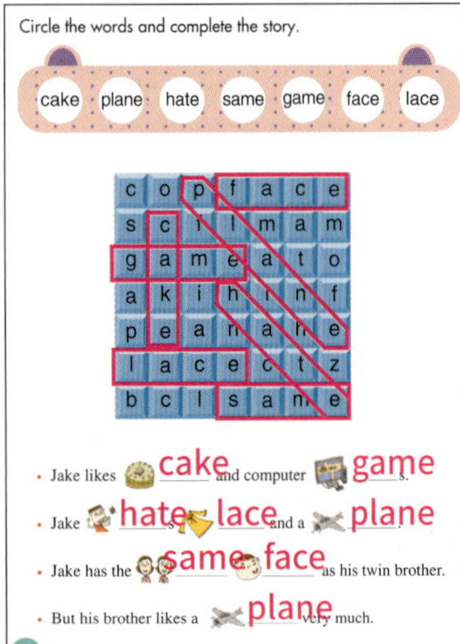

76p

❶ hike
   bike
❷ ride
   side
❸ smile
❹ pine
❺ bite
   kite
❻ five

77p

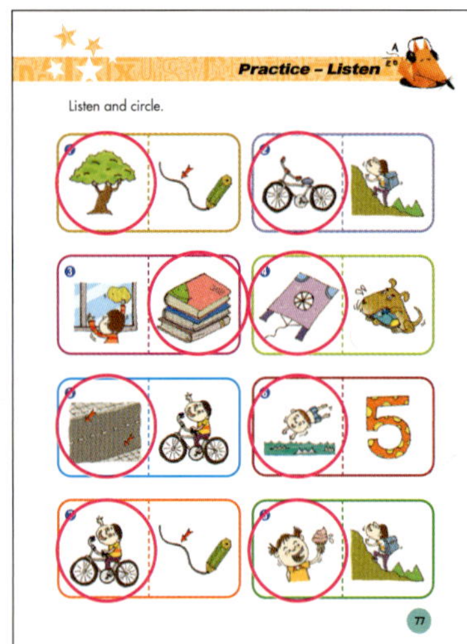

78p

❶ F
❷ F
❸ T
❹ T
❺ T
❻ T

79p

❶ bike
❷ bite
❸ kite
❹ pine
❺ ride
❻ hike
❼ five
❽ smile
❾ dive

80p

86p

❶ hole
   mole
❷ cone
   bone
❸ rope
❹ nose
   rose
❺ note
   vote

87p

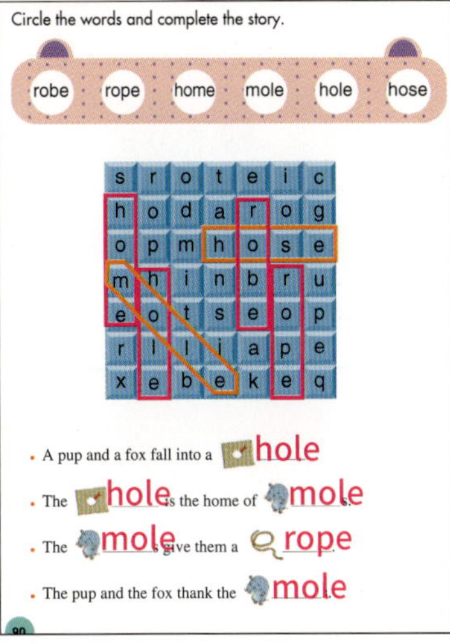

90p

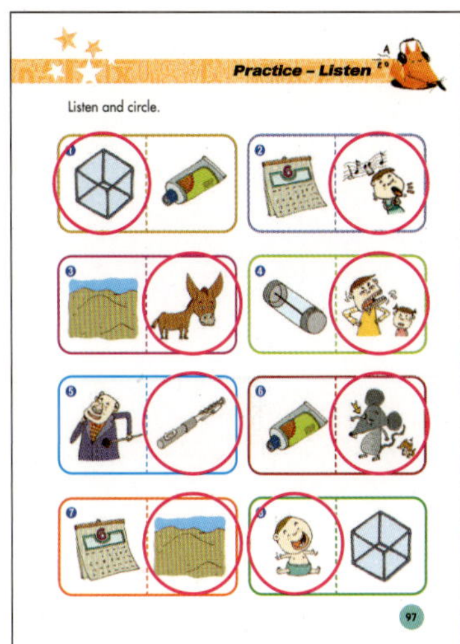

97p

88p
1. F
2. T
3. T
4. T
5. F
6. F

89p
1. hope
2. bone
3. hose
4. home
5. vote
6. cone
7. rose
8. rope
9. mole

96p
1. cube
   tube
2. dune
   June
   tune
3. rude
4. flute
   cute
5. mule

98p
1. T
2. F
3. T
4. T
5. T
6. F

99p
1. duke
2. cute
3. flute
4. rude
5. tube
6. cube
7. huge
8. June
9. tune

117

Answer Key

100p

Circle the words and complete the story.

hope	huge	cube	mule	cute	dune

- A **cute** kid is on the **mule** in the sand **dune**s.
- The kid is very hot and thirsty.
- But, there is no water in his bottle.
- His hope is to get a **huge** ice **cube**.

102p

❶ face ❷ nose
❸ cane ❹ kite
❺ pine ❻ cube
❼ lake

103p

❶ fl / t ❷ r / c
❸ d / v ❹ v / t
❺ d / n ❻ c / p

104p

105p

❶ same / face
❷ hike
❸ mole / hole
❹ bite
❺ gate
❻ hate

Test

106p

❶ c ❷ a
❸ a ❹ b
❺ a ❻ c

107p

Find and circle the words.

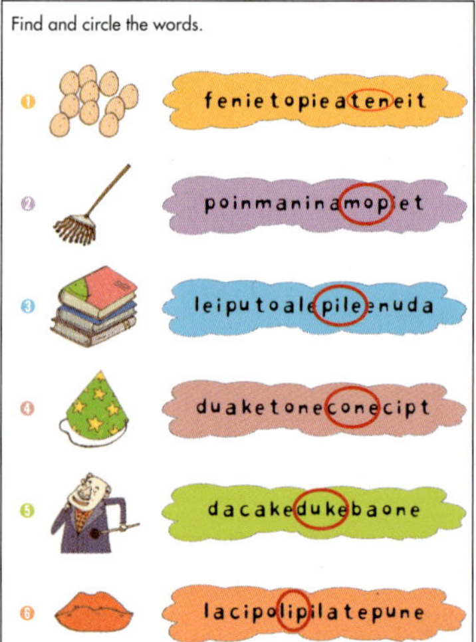

108p

❶ b ❷ a
❸ c ❹ c
❺ a ❻ c
❼ b ❽ b
❾ c ❿ c
⓫ b ⓬ a

118

110p

❶ van

❷ flute

❸ like

❹ lace

❺ hope

❻ sun

111p

❶ pot

❷ hen / sad

❸ vase / cape

❹ big / kite

❺ pup / hut

❻ hole

alphabet & words

ANT

BEAR

CROCODILE

DUCK

ELEPHANT

FOX

GIRAFFE

HARE

IGUANA

JELLYFISH

KANGAROO

LION

MOUSE

NIGHTINGALE

OWL

PIG

QUAIL

RACCOON

SQUIRREL

TIGER

UNICORN

VARAN

WOLF

X-RAY FISH

YAK

ZEBRA

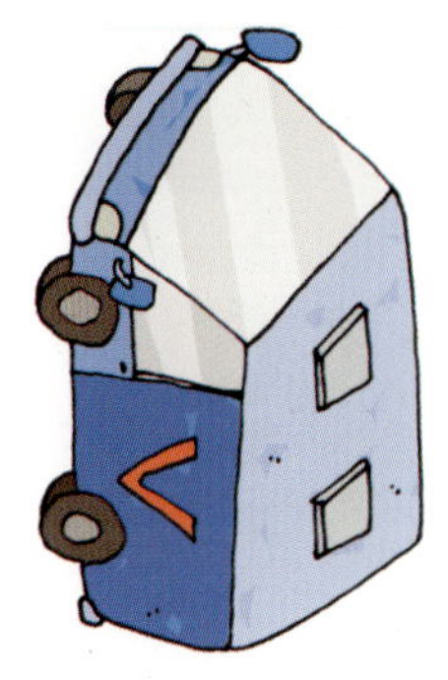

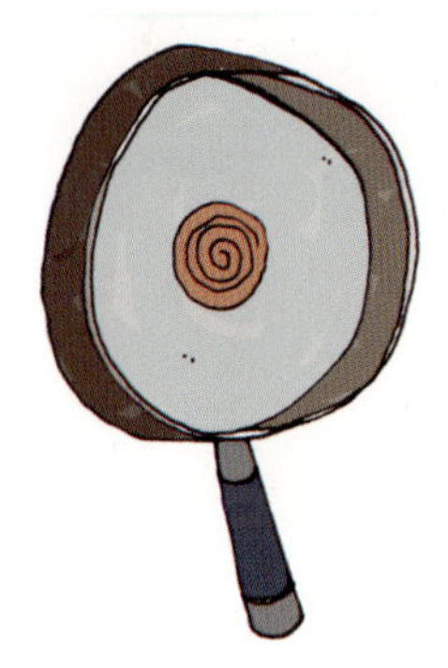

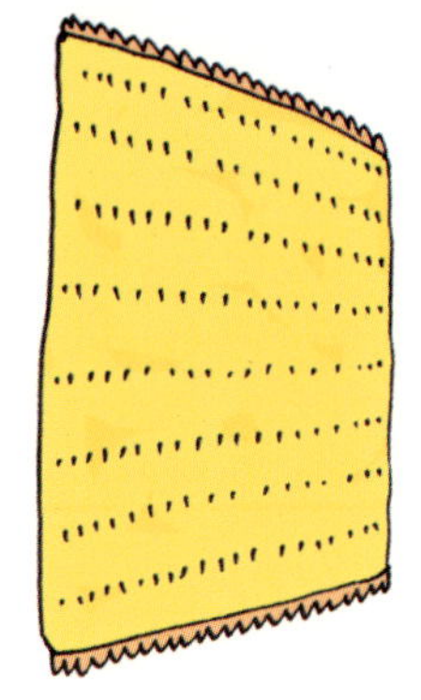

ham

jam

ram

man

pan

nap

van

cap

lap

mat

rat

fat

dad

bad

sad

bed

kid	net	ten	red
lid	jet	hen	wed
big	wet	pen	leg
pig	bib	men	egg

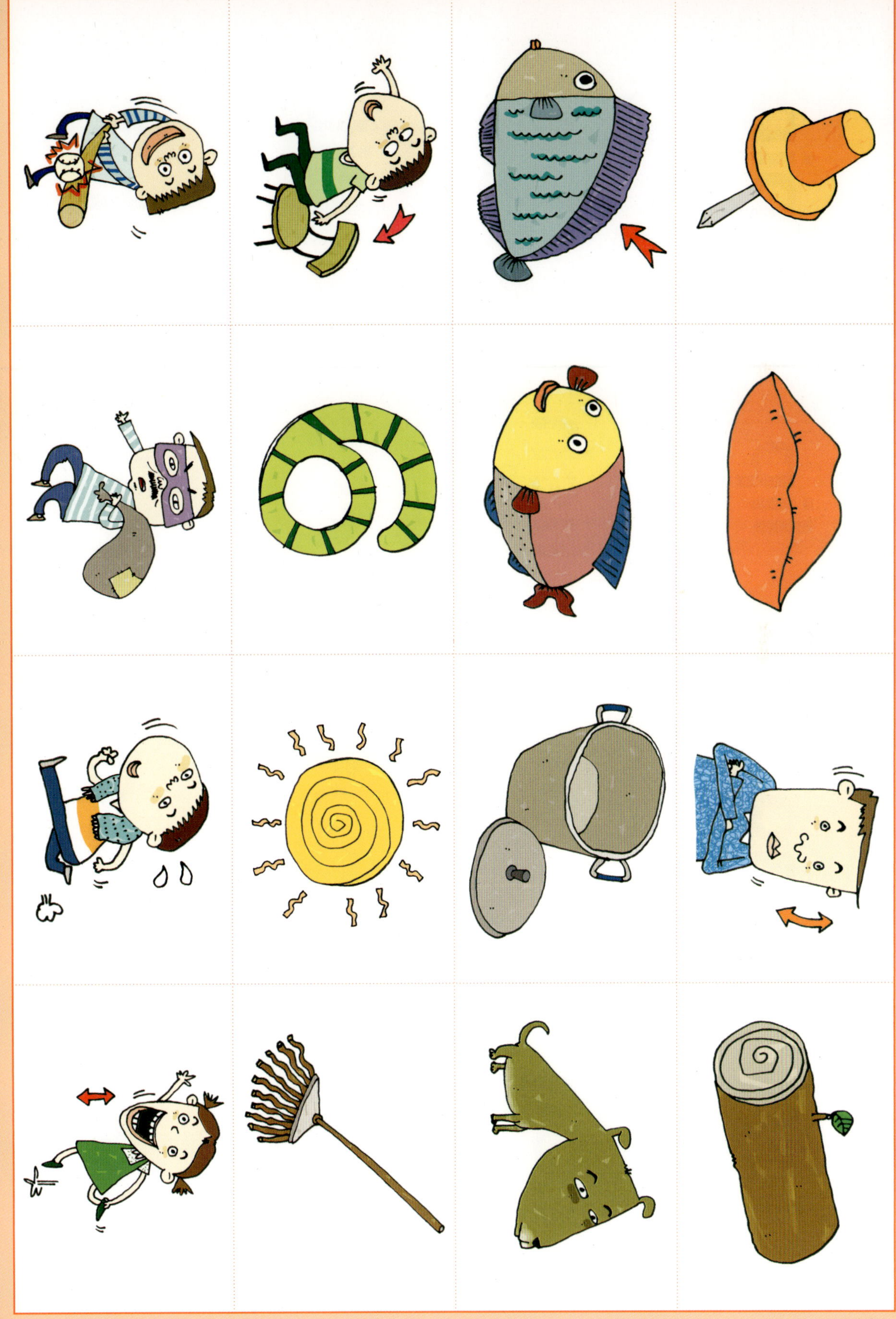

log	nod	lip	pin
dog	pot	fish	fin
mop	hot	six	sit
hop	jog	rob	hit

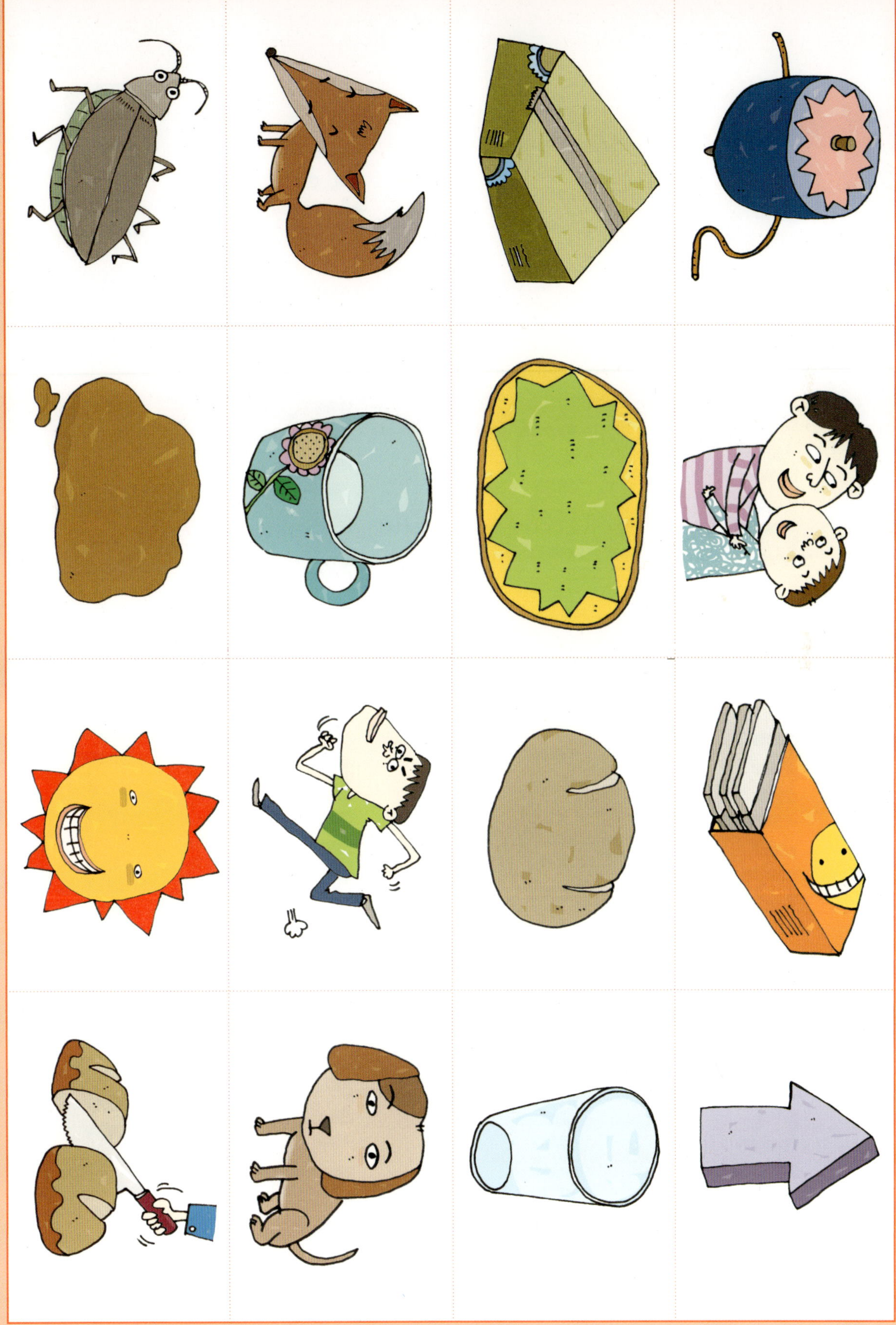

up	gum	hug	top
cup	bun	rug	box
pup	run	mug	fox
cut	sun	mud	bug

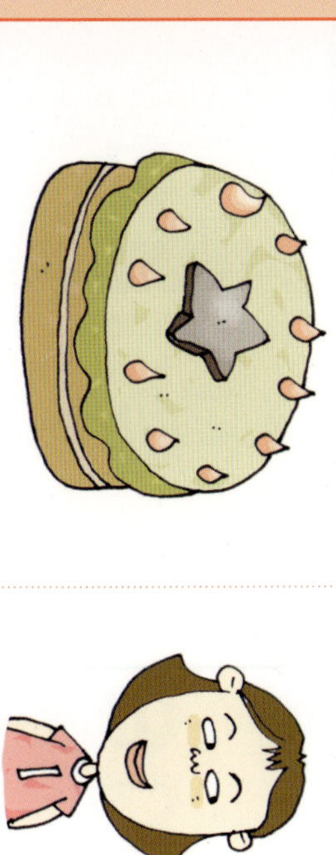
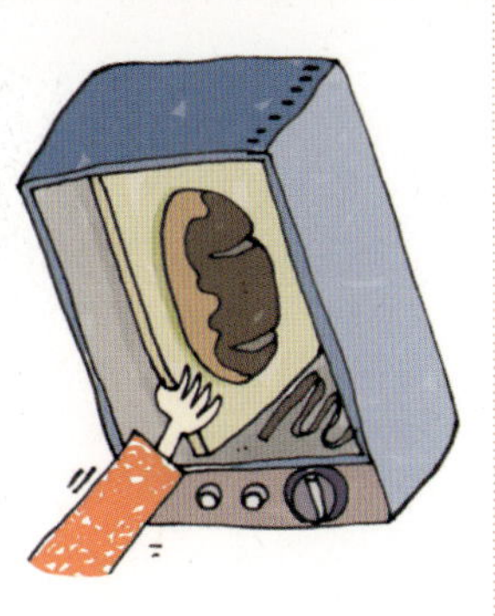
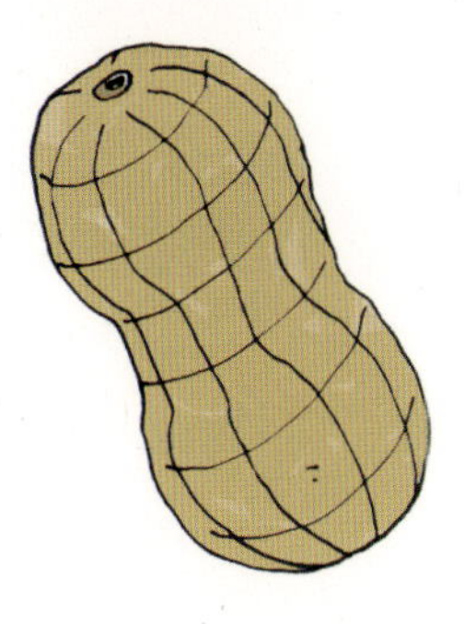
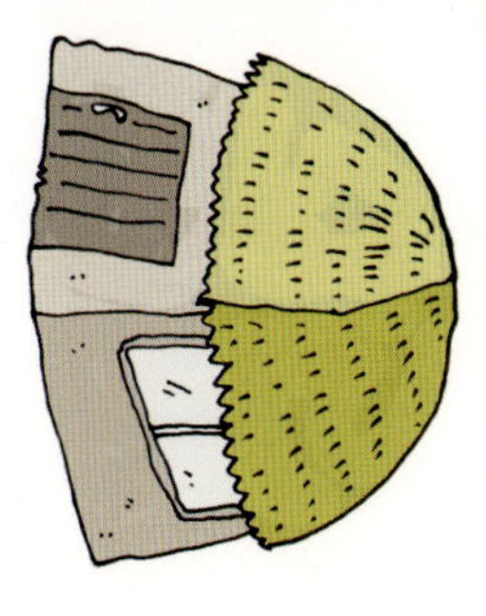
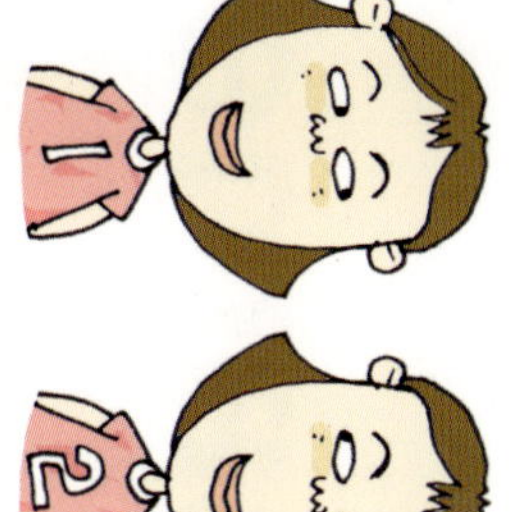

Nana

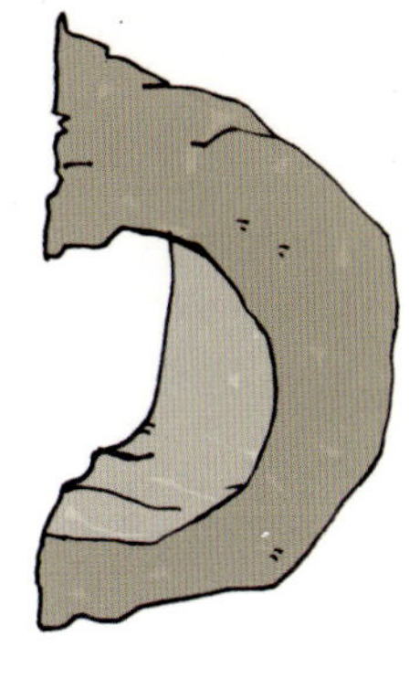

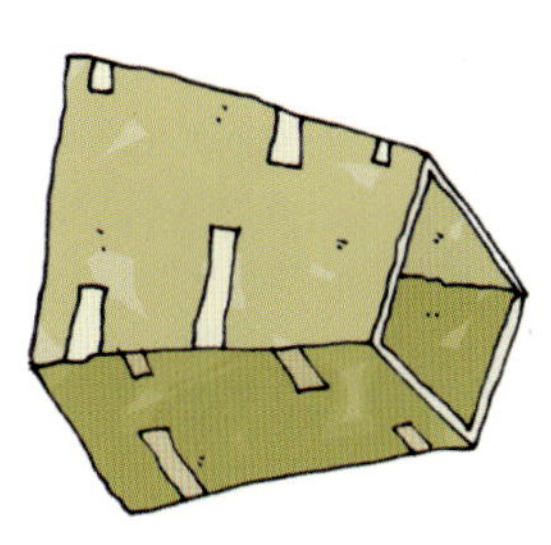

wave	lace	lake	hut
vase	race	name	nut
case	face	game	bake
tape	cave	same	cake

smile	line	plane	cape
wipe	bike	mane	gate
pile	like	bite	hate
kite	hike	pine	cane

pole	vote	nose	side
hole	note	rose	ride
mole	bone	rope	dive
home	cone	hope	five

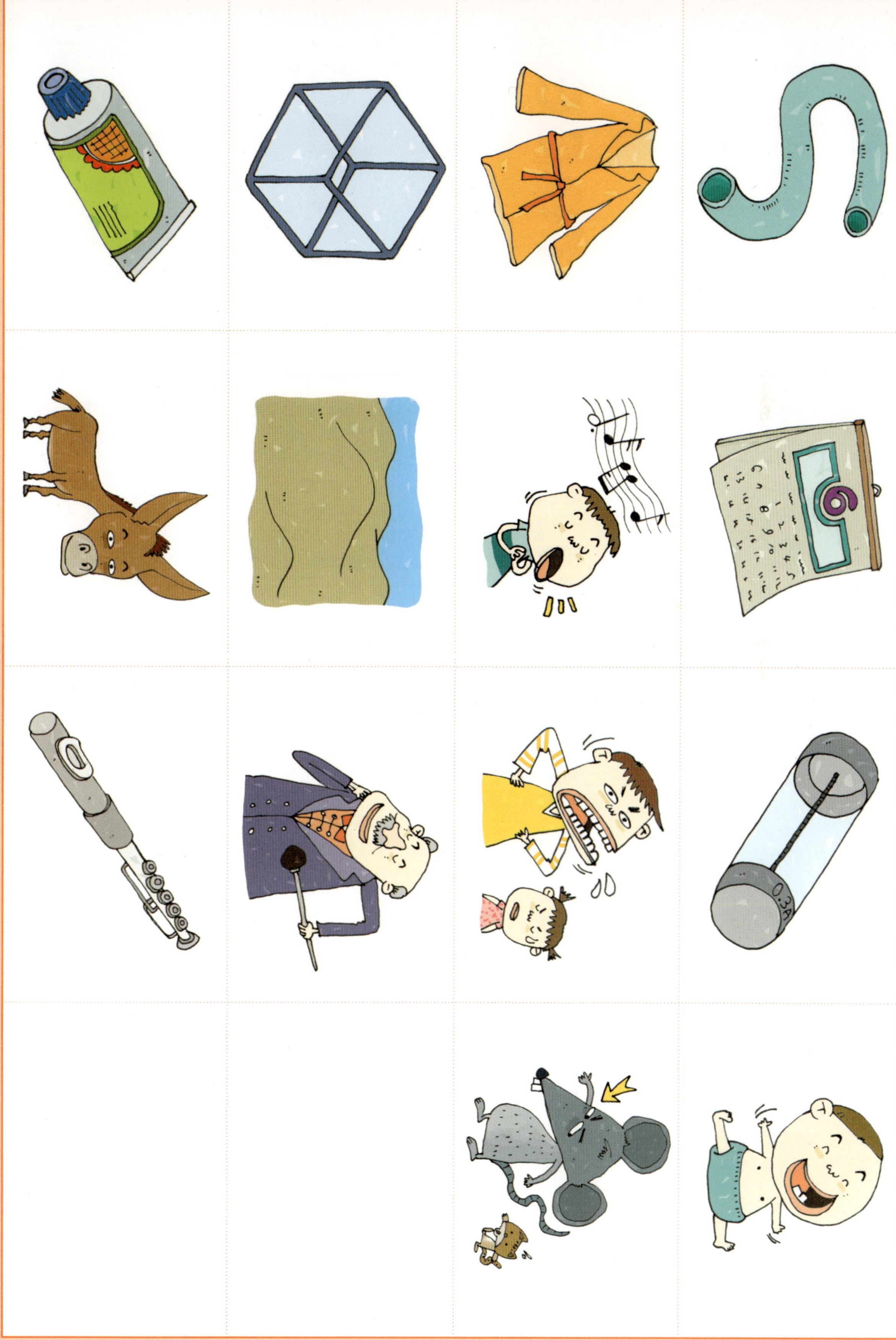

hose

robe

cube

tube

June

tune

dune

mule

fuse

rude

duke

flute

cute

huge

JUMP UP

Phonics

개정판 **2**

Short Vowels / Long Vowels ★ Workbook

International Linguistics Research Institute

CONTENTS

Unit 1   Short Vowel **a**

A Circle and Write.

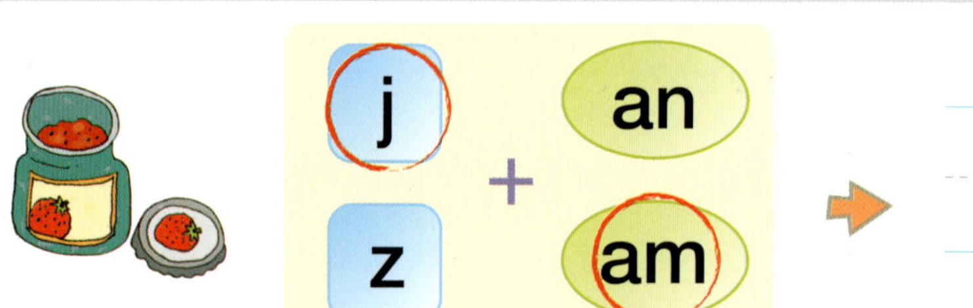

| j + am → | jam |

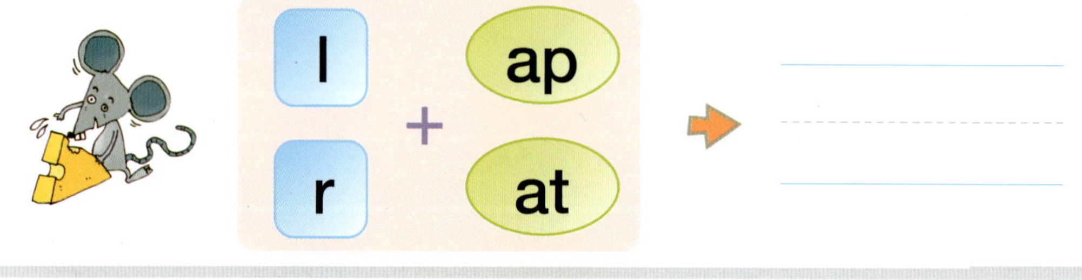

B Check the right pictures.

ram

fat

nap

man

sad

ham

C Match the words with the pictures.

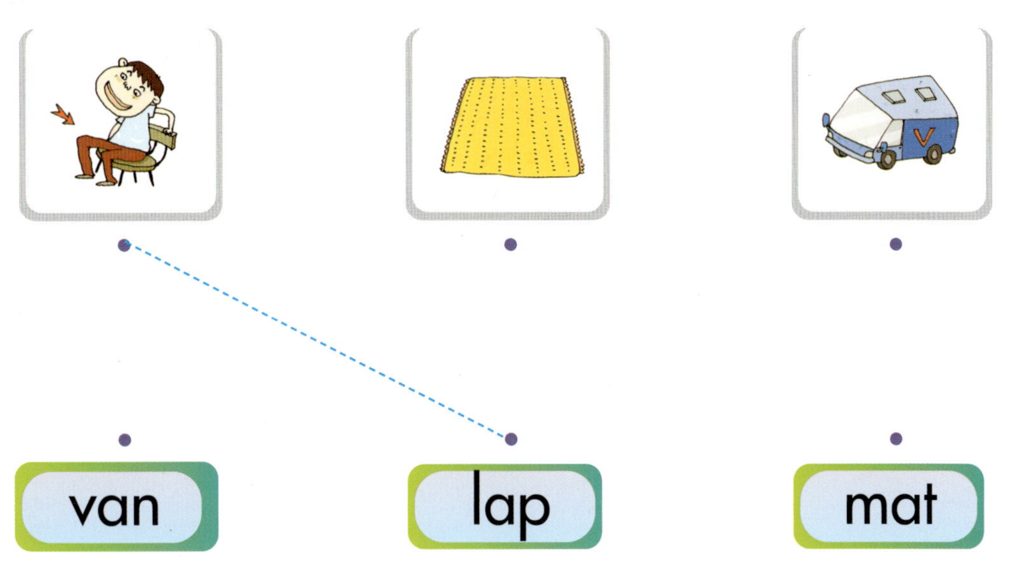

van

lap

mat

D Write the correct letters.

 b a d

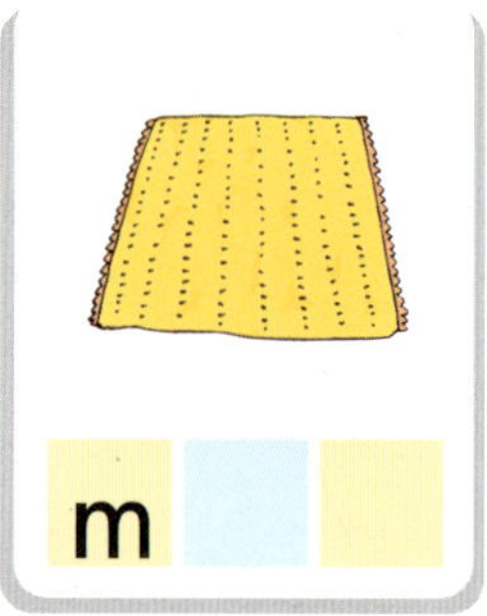 m ☐ ☐

 l ☐ ☐

 p ☐ ☐

 h ☐ ☐

 s ☐ ☐

 f ☐ ☐

 n ☐ ☐

E Match and Color.

van   ram   rat

F Circle the pictures that rhyme with the first pictures.

G Circle the pictures that rhyme is Not same.

h a m

Unit 2 Short Vowel e

A Circle and Write.

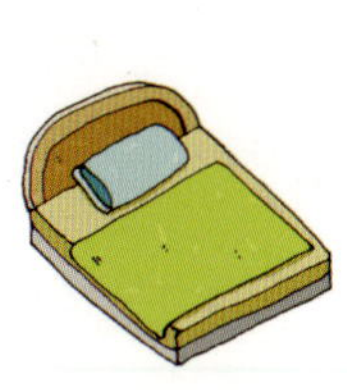 b / d + eg / ed 

 r / l + en / eg 

 p / t + et / en

 z / j + et / ed

 n / m + et / ed 

B Check the right pictures.

red

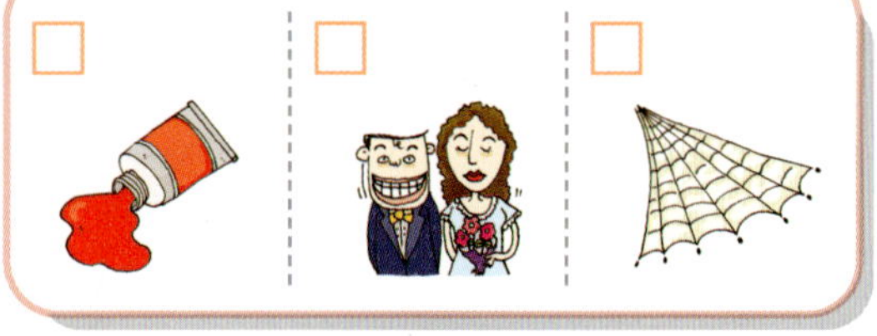

ten

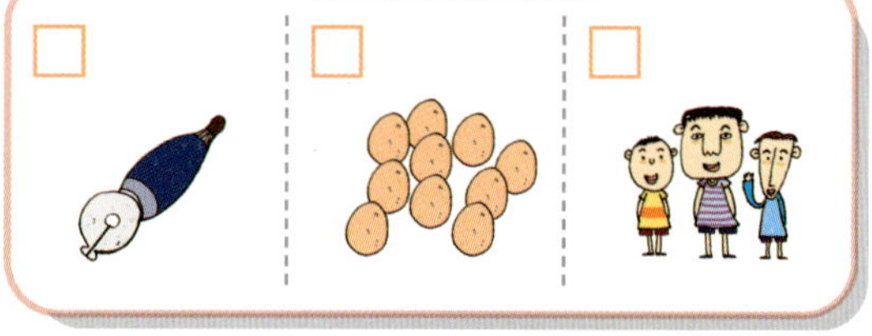

men

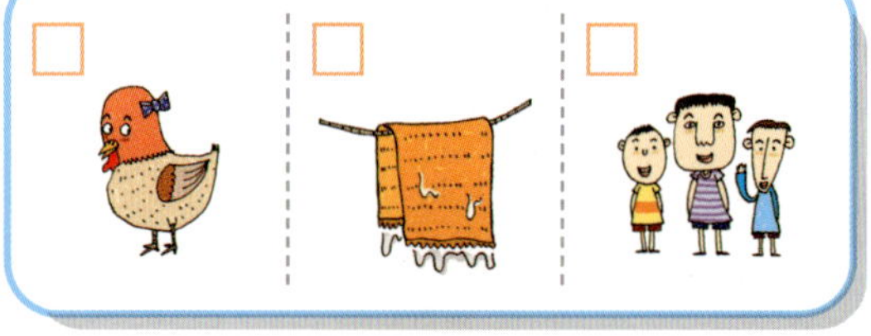

wet

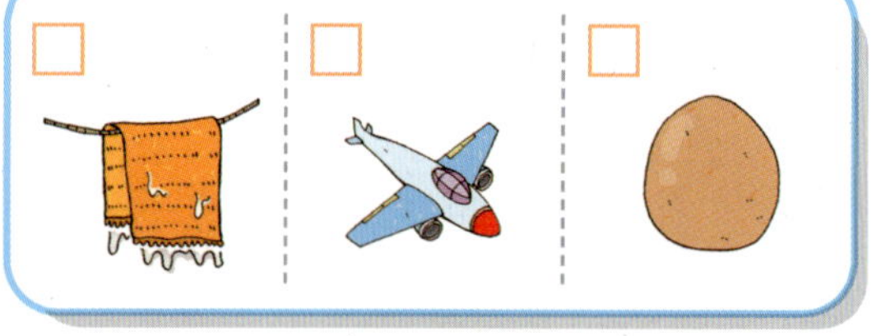

egg

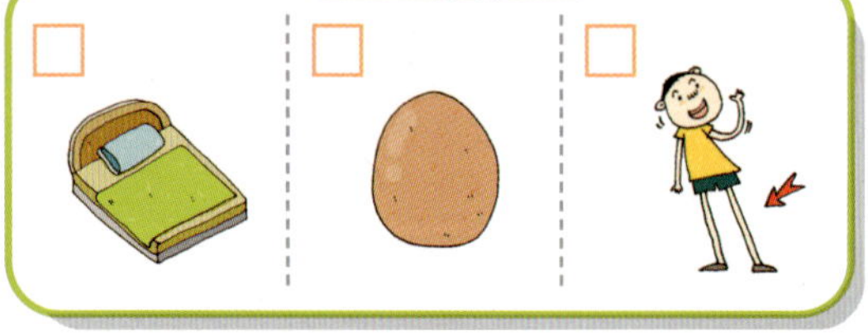

wed

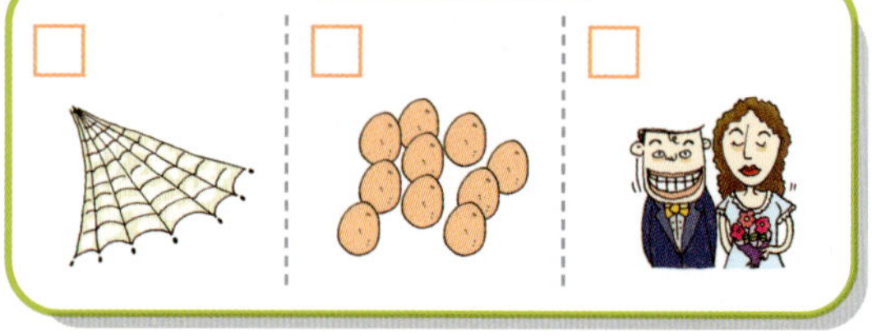

C Match the words with the pictures.

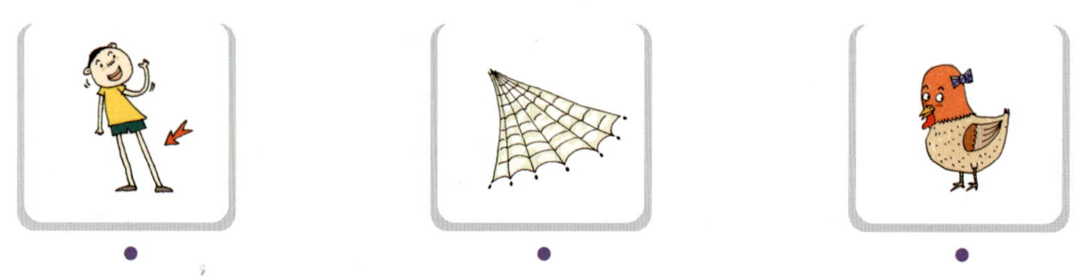

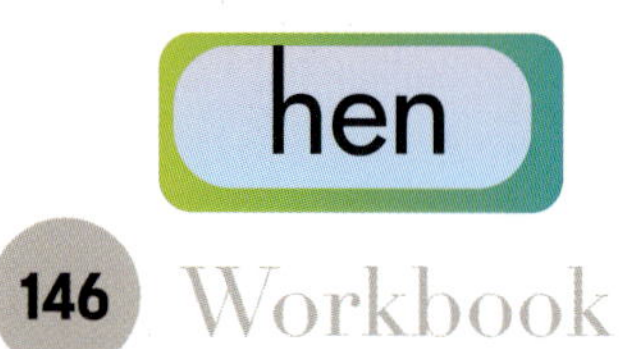

hen

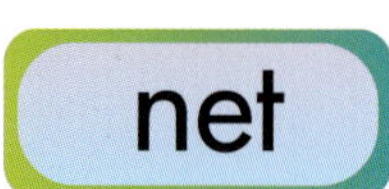

net

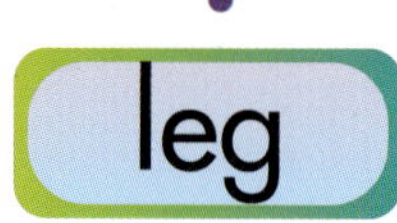

leg

D Write the correct letters.

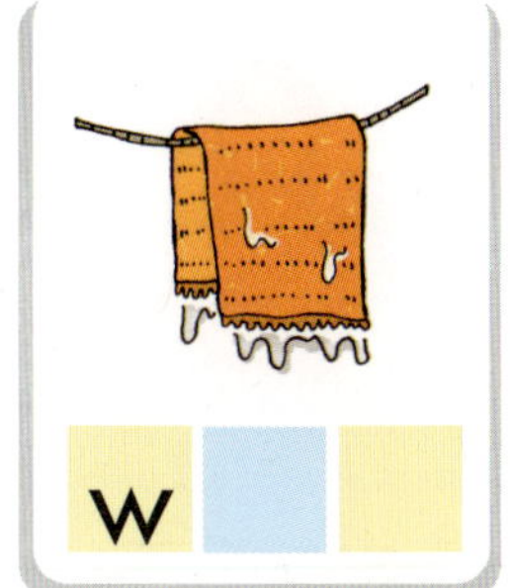
w

p

h

w

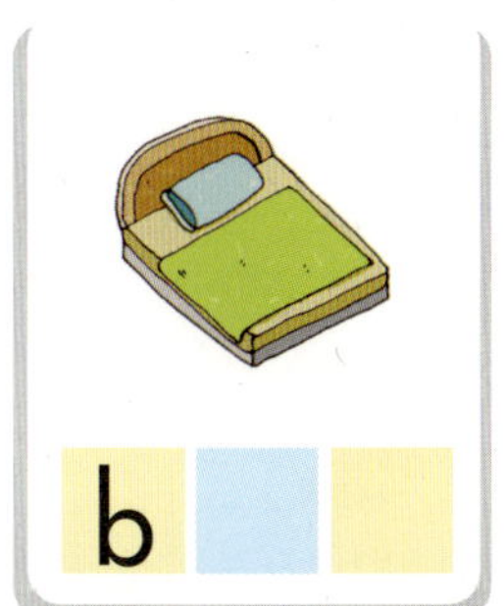
b

n

m

l

E Match and Color.

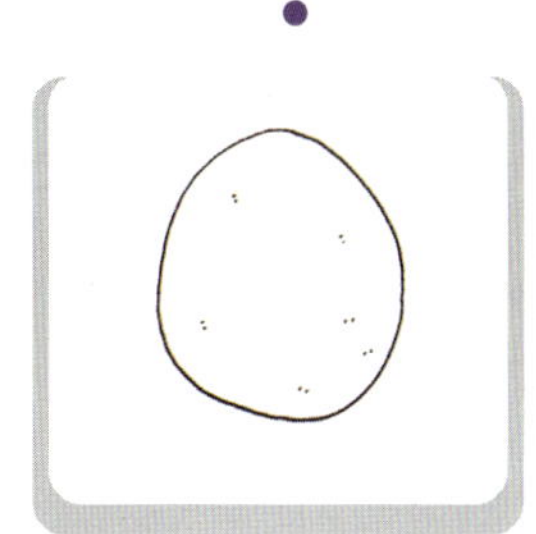

F Circle the pictures that rhyme with the first pictures.

G Circle the pictures that rhyme is Not same.

H Look and Write.

Unit 3   Short Vowel i

A Circle and Write.

c / k + ib / id

→ __________

q / p + ig / in

→ __________

p / f + id / in

→ __________

h / p + ix / it

→ __________

r / l + ip / ig

→ __________

B Check the right pictures.

bib

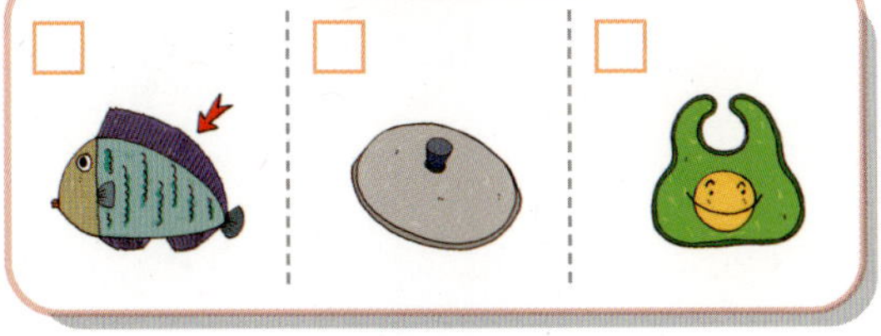

big

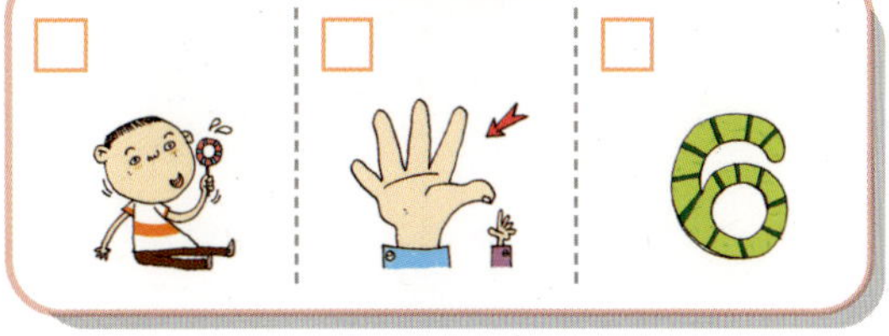

fish

pin

six

lid

C Match the words with the pictures.

sit

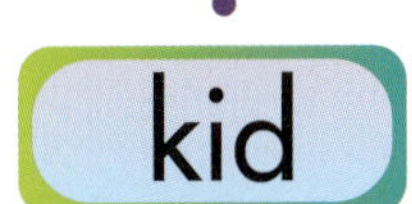
kid

fin

D Write the correct letters.

p
b
p
h
l
s
k
f

E Match and Color.

sit

lid

big

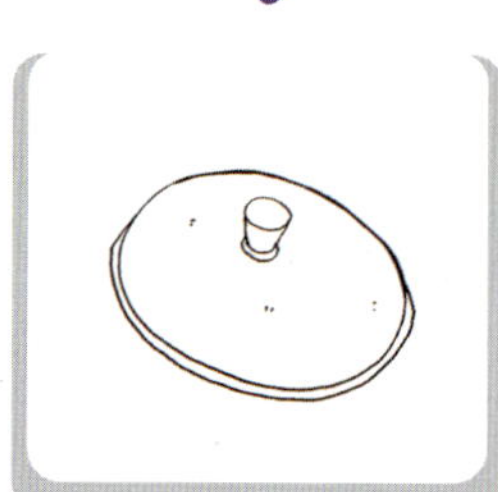

F Circle the pictures that rhyme with the first pictures.

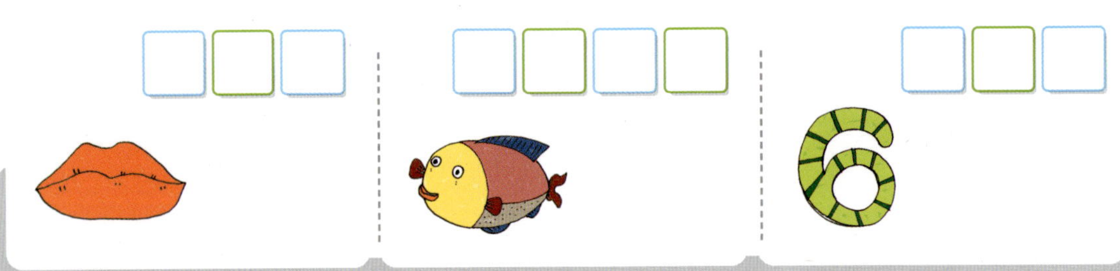

Unit 4 — Short Vowel O

A Circle and Write.

 | h / p + op / ot → 

 | v / d + og / ob → 

 | t / k + op / og → 

 | l / n + ob / od → 

 | f / b + ox / ot → 

B Check the right pictures.

rob

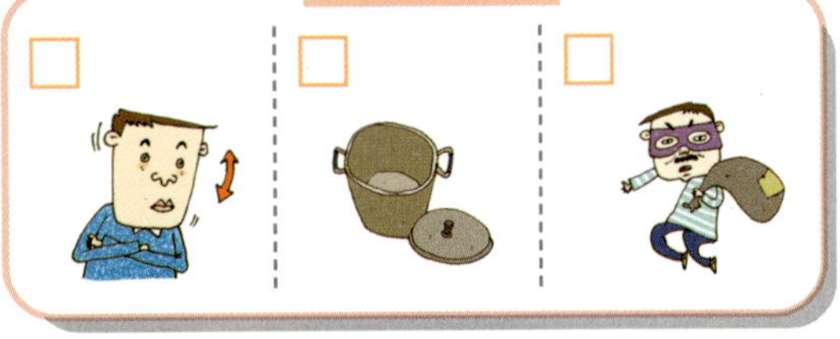

log

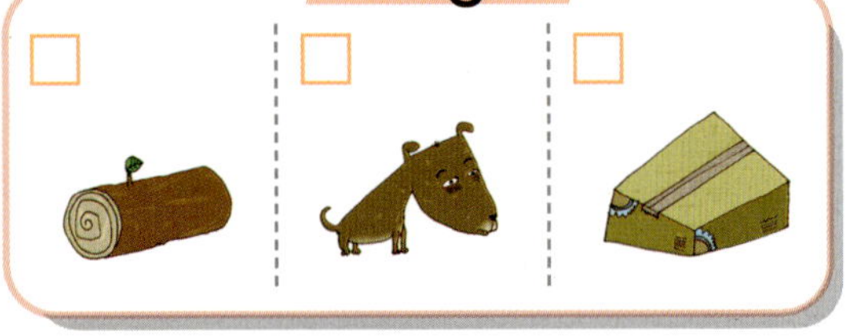

pot

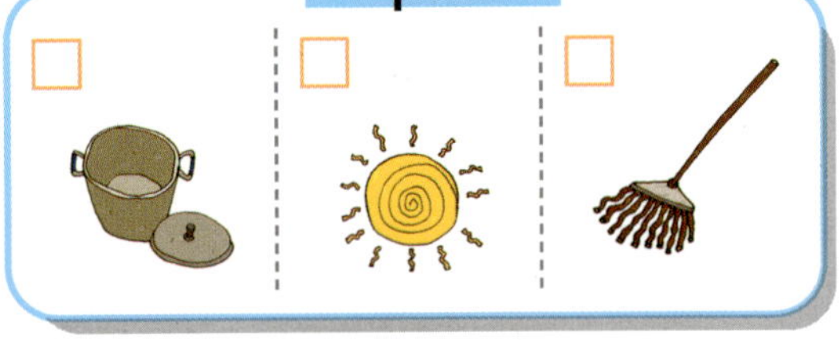

hop

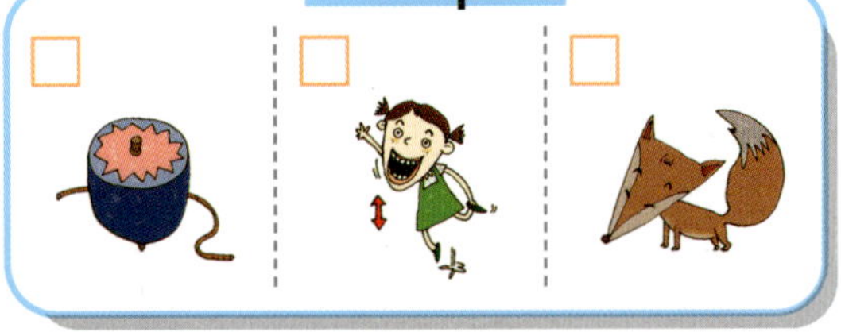

fox

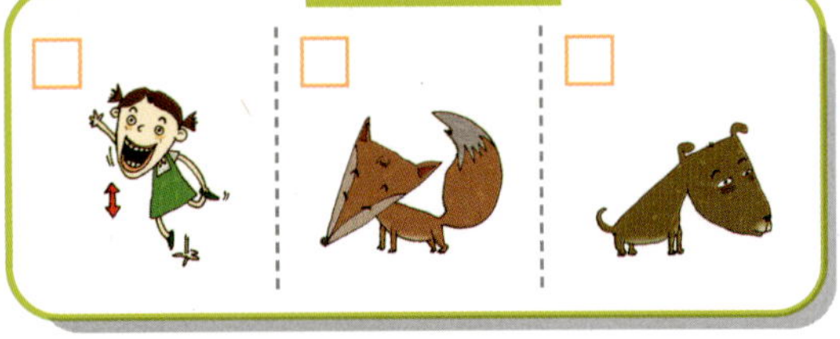

nod

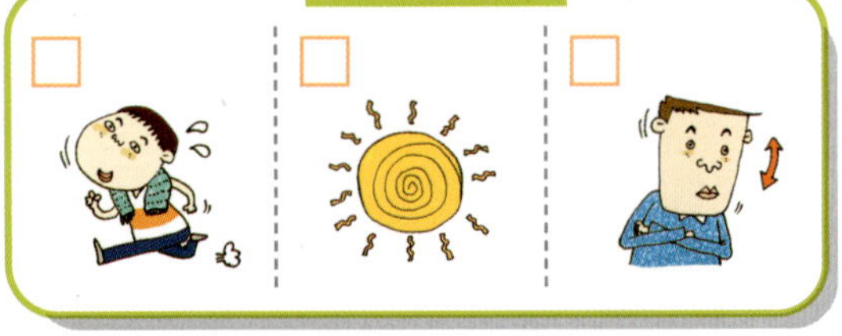

C Match the words with the pictures.

mop

jog

rob

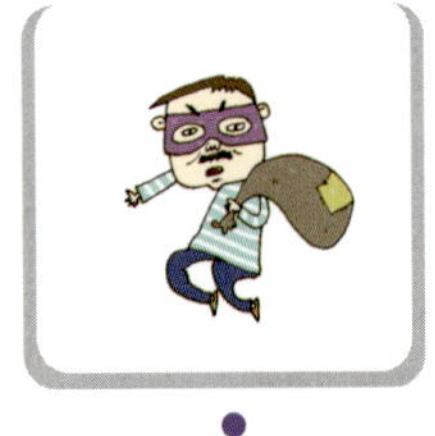

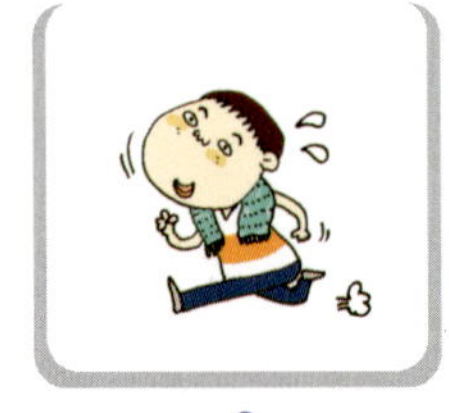

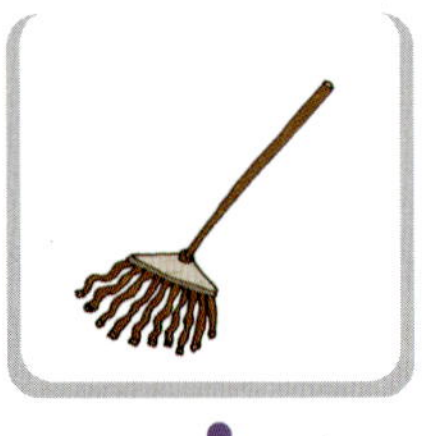

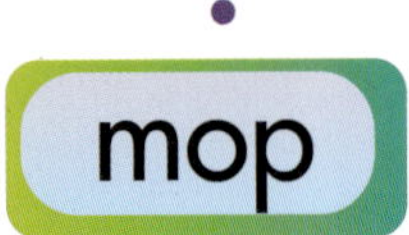

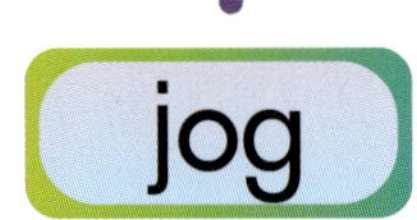

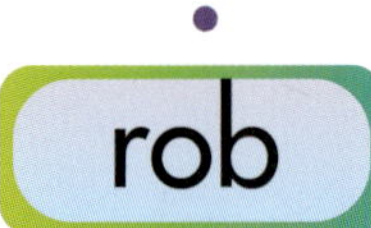

D Write the correct letters.

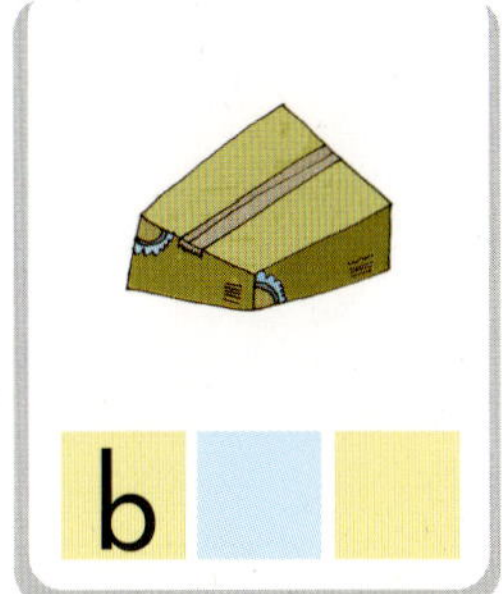

b ▢ ▢

h ▢ ▢

l ▢ ▢

p ▢ ▢

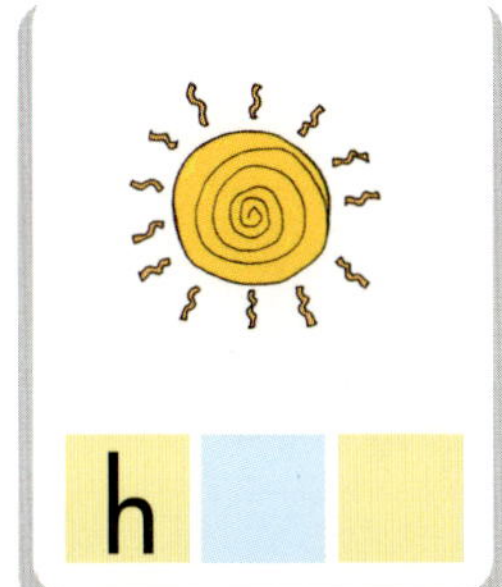

h ▢ ▢

j ▢ ▢

t ▢ ▢

r ▢ ▢

E Match and Color.

fox

top

dog

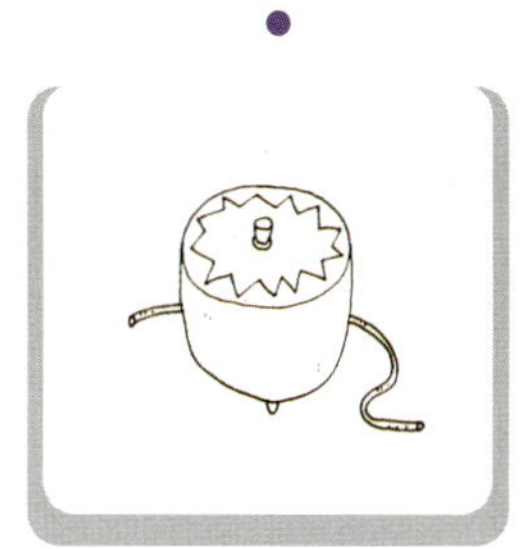

 Circle the pictures that rhyme with the first pictures.

 Circle the pictures that rhyme is Not same.

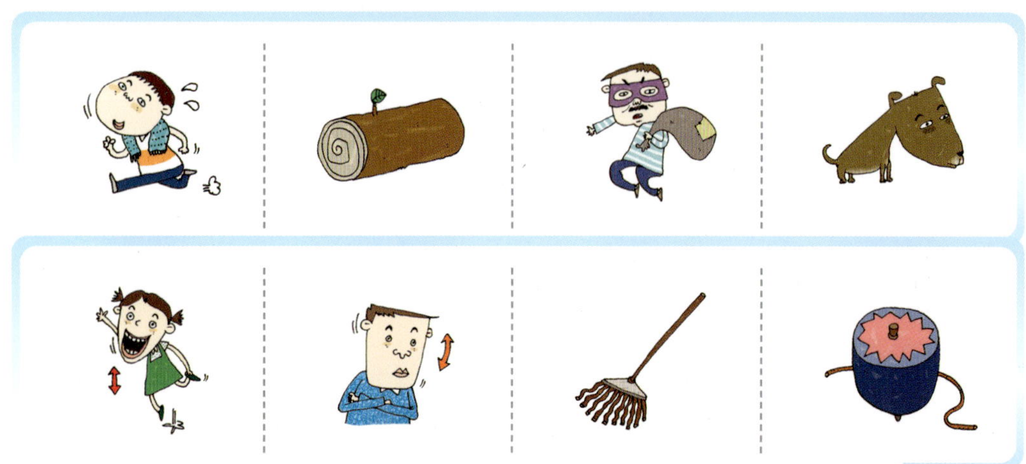

H Look and Write.

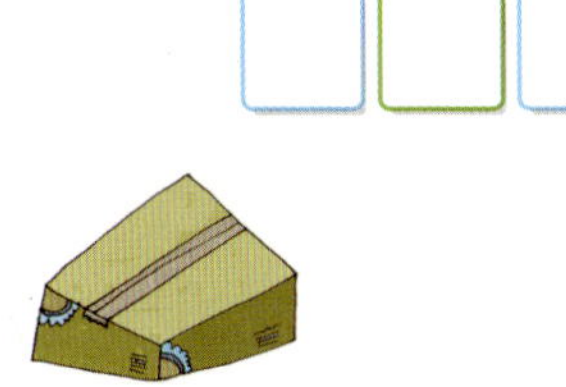

Unit 5 Short Vowel u

A Circle and Write.

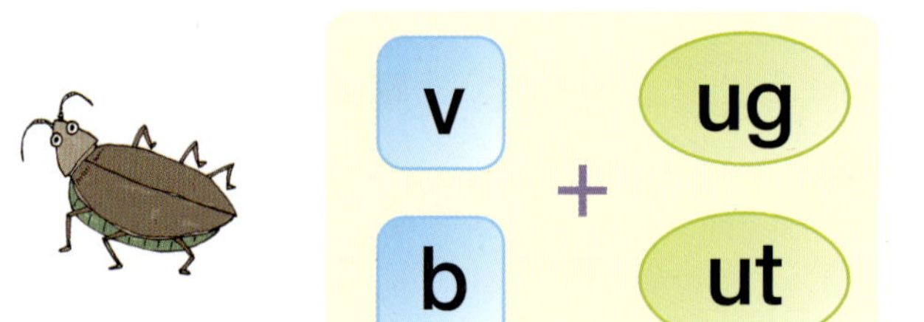

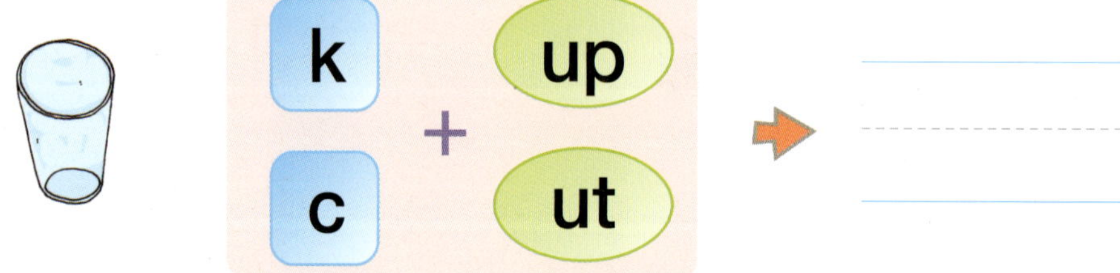

B Check the right pictures.

hug

gum

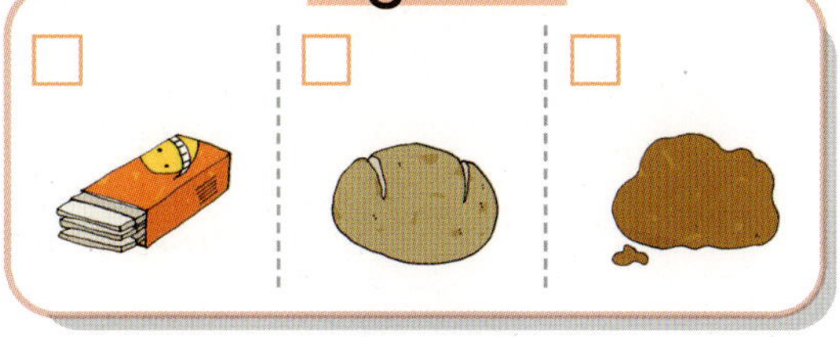

nut

up

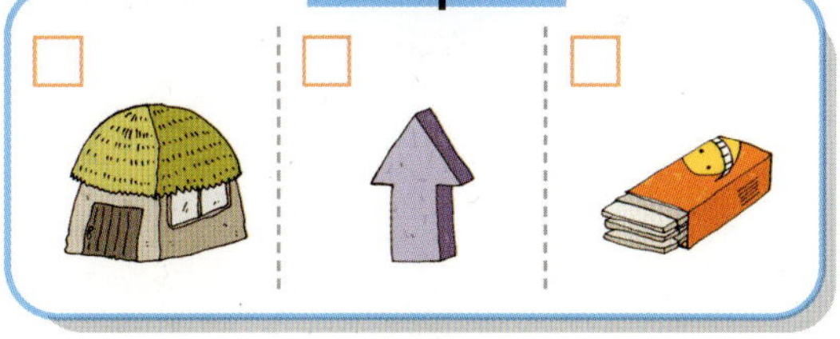

run

rug

C Match the words with the pictures.

cut

pup

bun

 Write the correct letters.

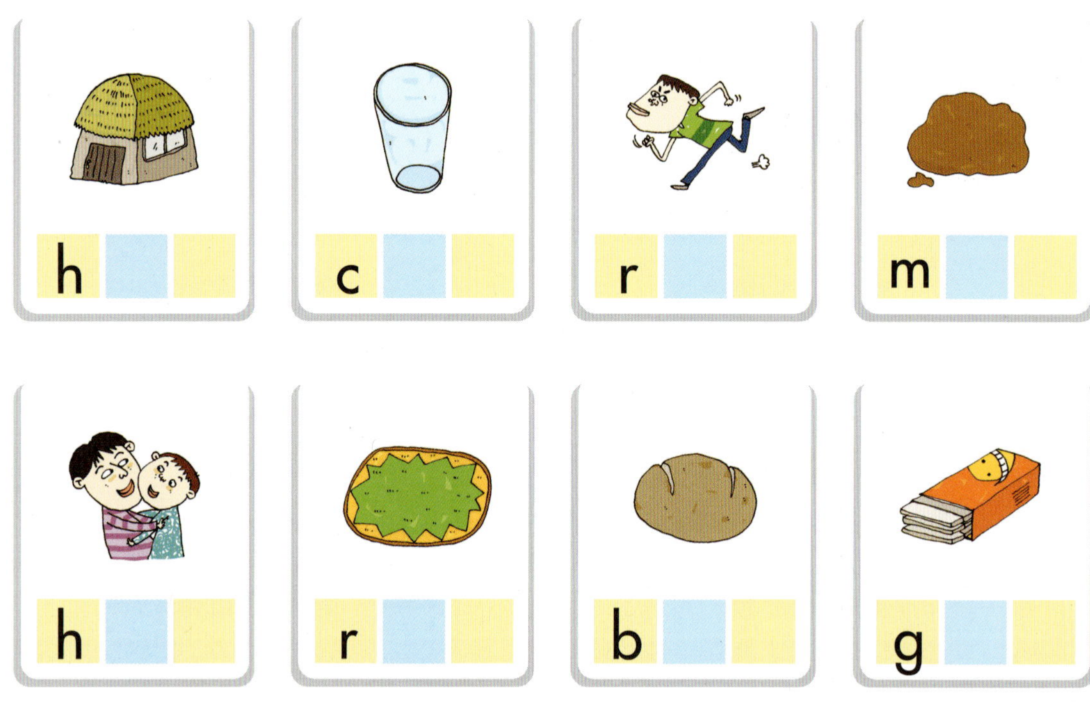

 Match and Color.

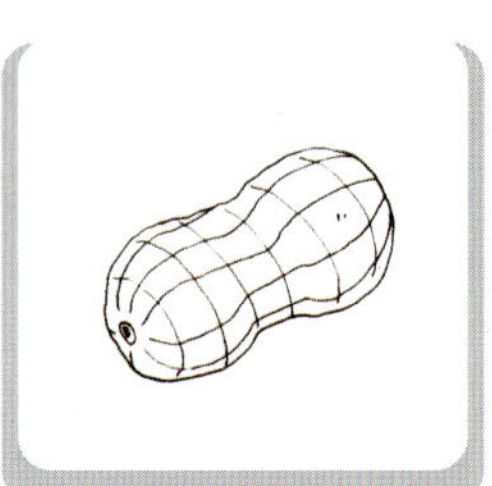

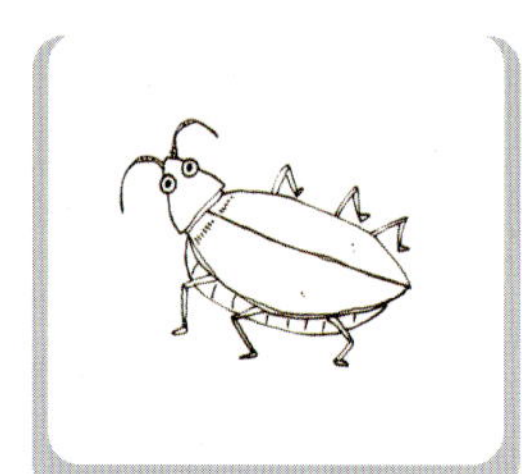

F Circle the pictures that rhyme with the first pictures.

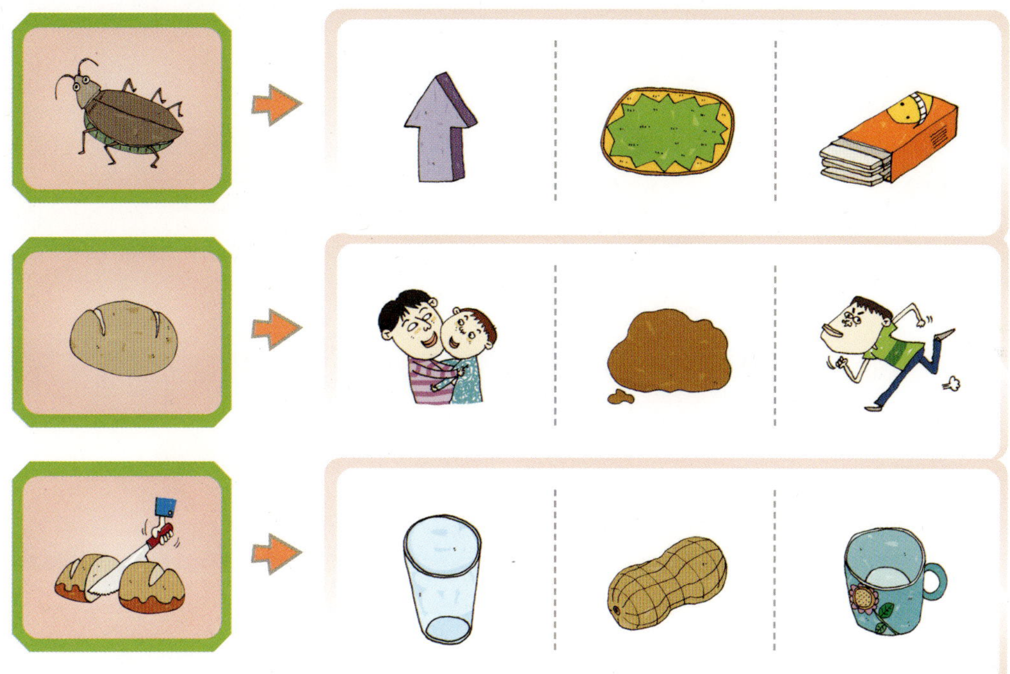

G Circle the pictures that rhyme is Not same.

H Look and Write.

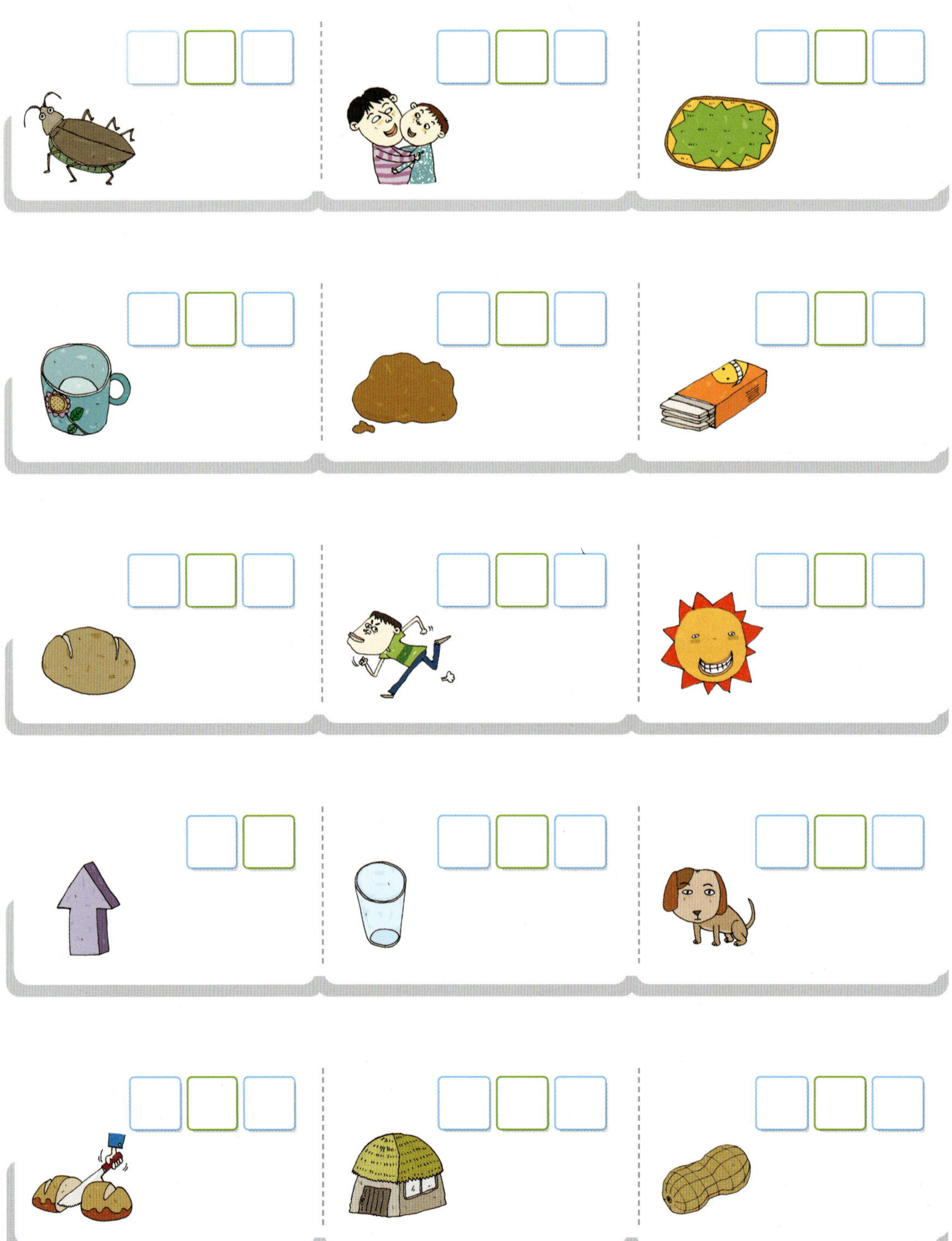

A Circle the pictures with the match sounds.

short **a** sound

 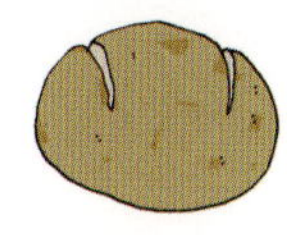  

short **e** sound

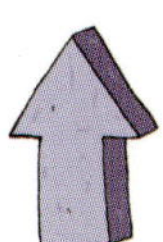 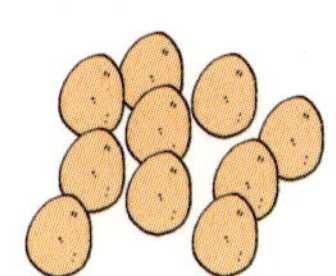  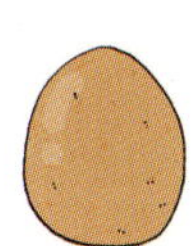

short **i** sound

short **o** sound

short **u** sound

B Look and Match.

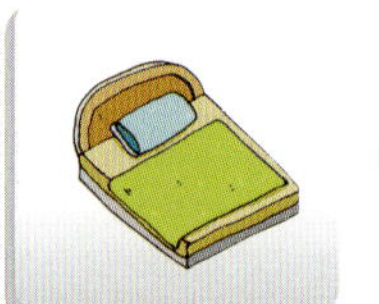  -at 

  -ed 

  -id 

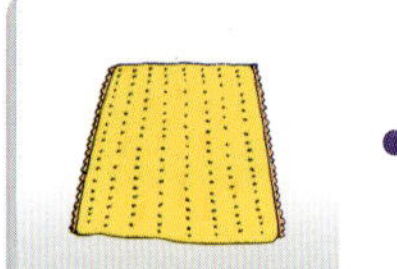  -ot 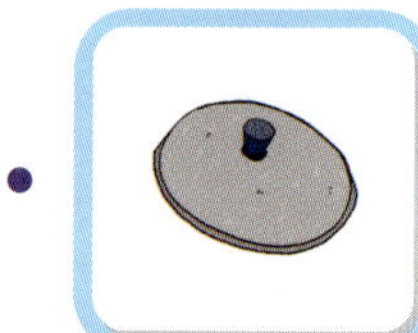

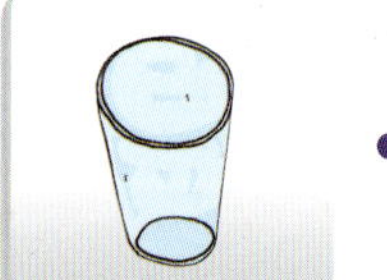  -up 

  -in 

C Match the right picture.

 jam   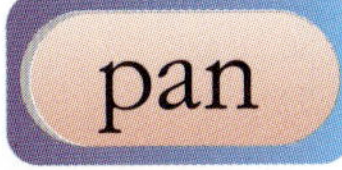 pan    cap   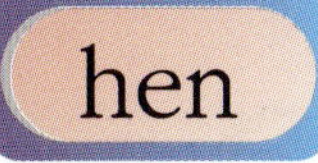 hen

 jet    big    sit   log

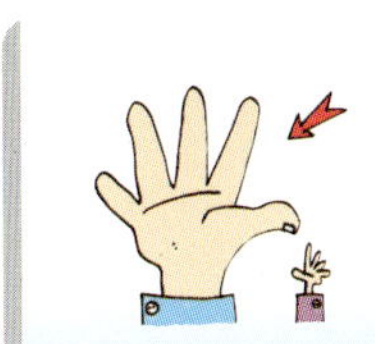   

D Check the right words.

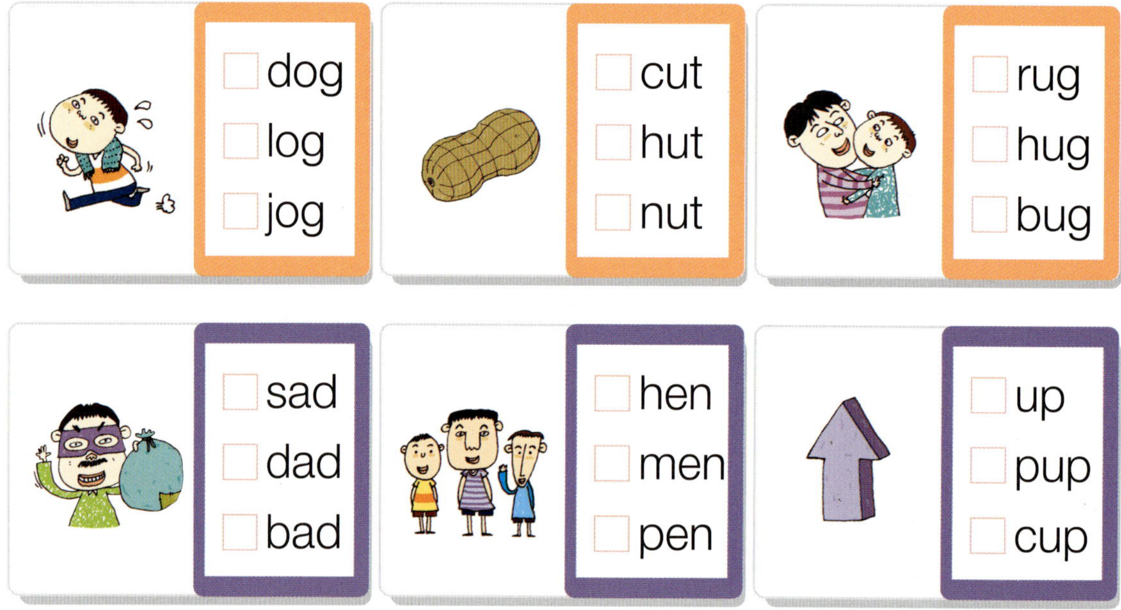
□ dog
□ log
□ jog

□ cut
□ hut
□ nut

□ rug
□ hug
□ bug

□ sad
□ dad
□ bad

□ hen
□ men
□ pen

□ up
□ pup
□ cup

E Write the correct letters.

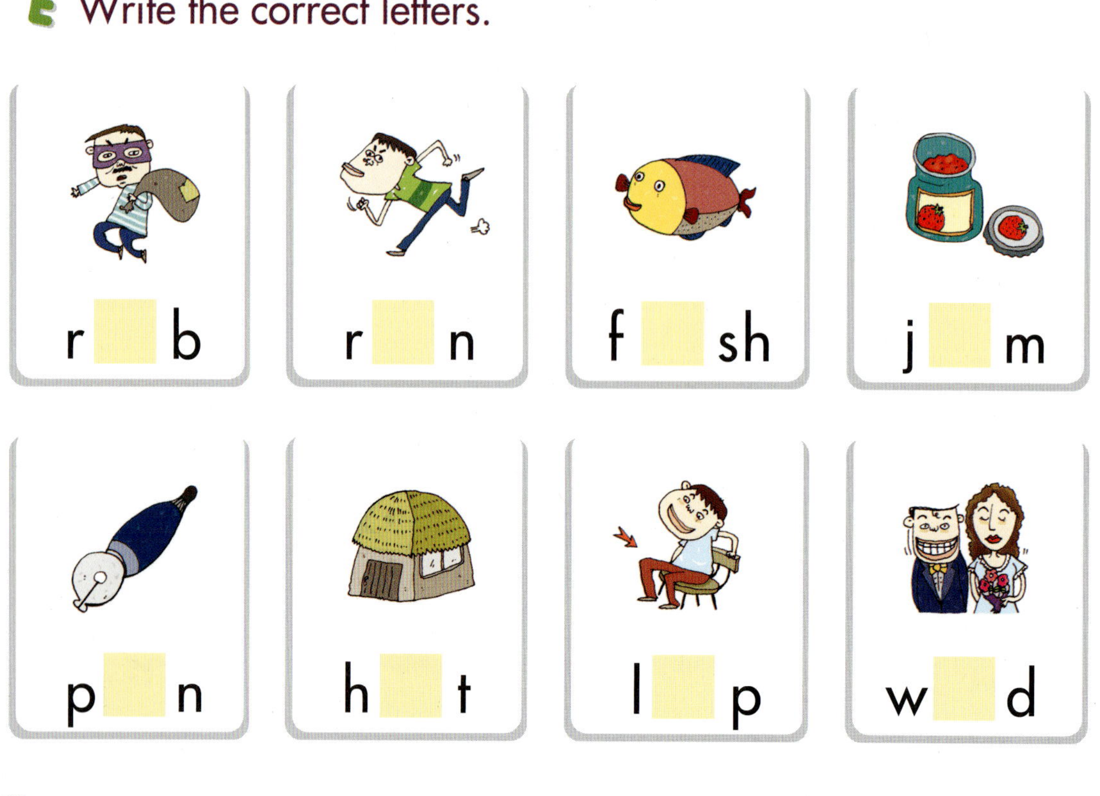
r _ b
r _ n
f _ sh
j _ m
p _ n
h _ t
l _ p
w _ d

F Look and Write.

jet

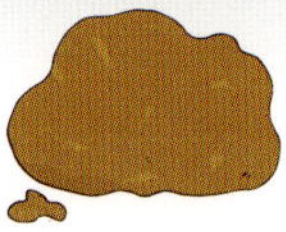

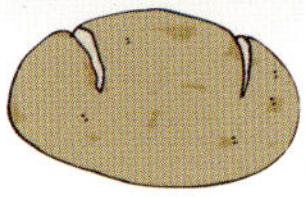

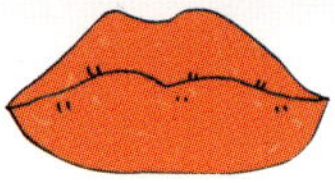

Unit 6 Long Vowel a

A Circle and Write.

c + ate
b + ake
→

k + ane
g + ame
→

 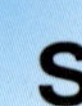

c + ase
s + ave
→

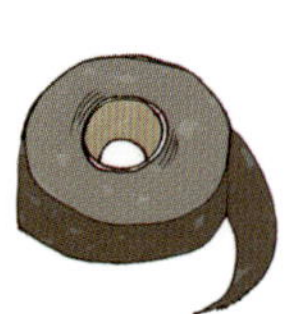

t + ate
c + ape
→

f + ase
v + ace
→ 

B Check the right pictures.

lake

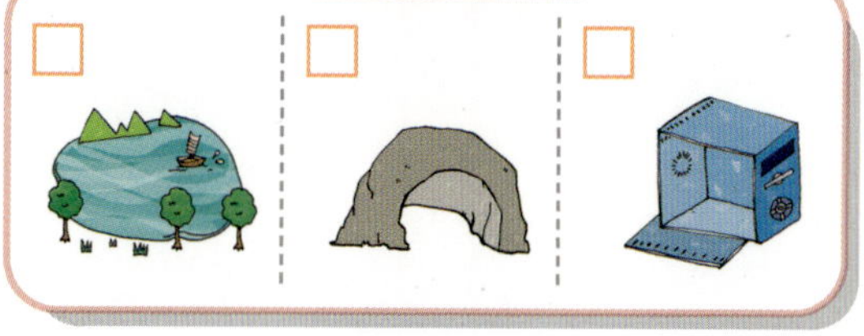

vase

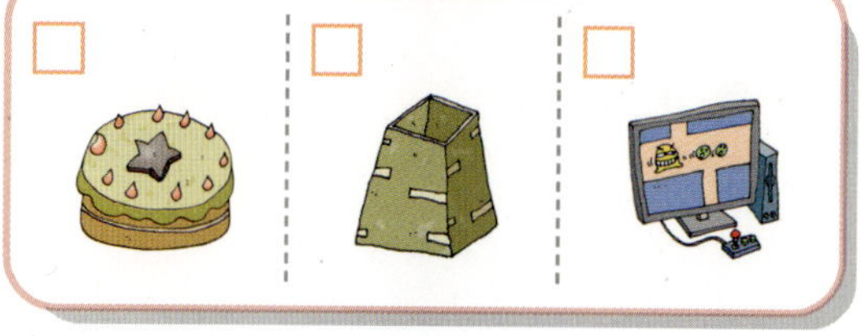

name

race

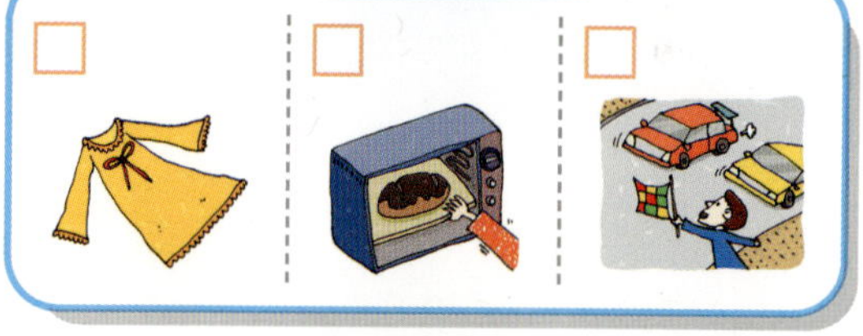

gate

mane

C Match the words with the pictures.

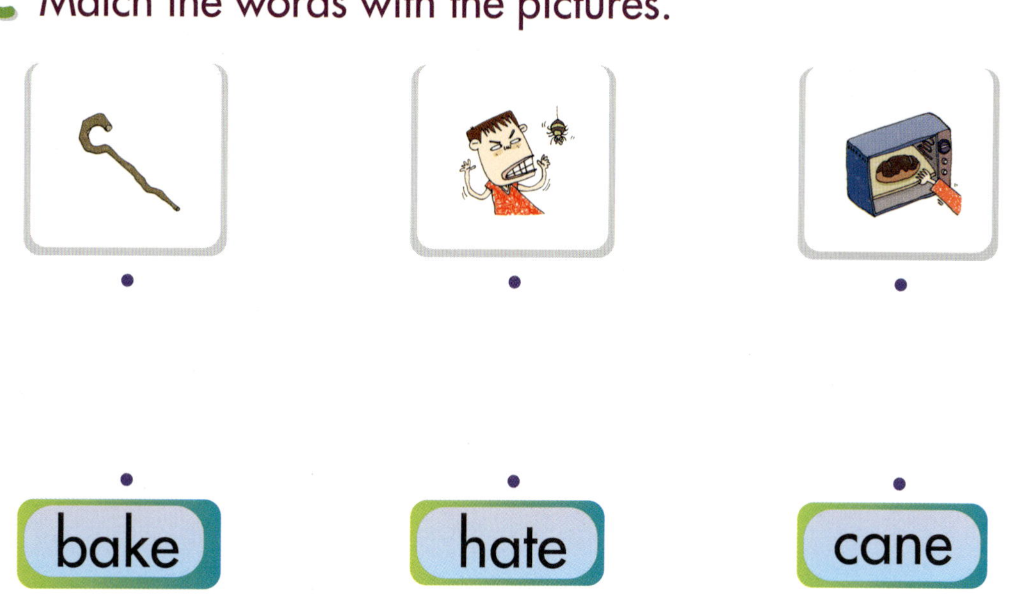

bake

hate

cane

 Write the correct letters.

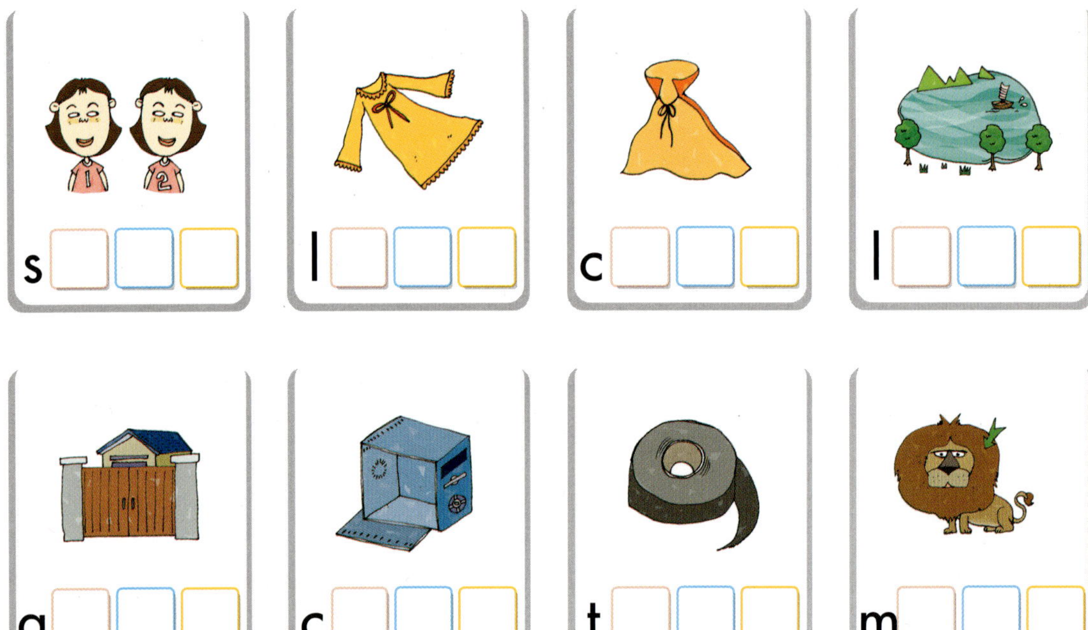

s □ □ □   l □ □ □   c □ □ □   l □ □ □

g □ □ □   c □ □ □   t □ □ □   m □ □ □

E **Match and Color.**

F Circle the pictures that rhyme with the first pictures.

G Circle the pictures that rhyme is Not same.

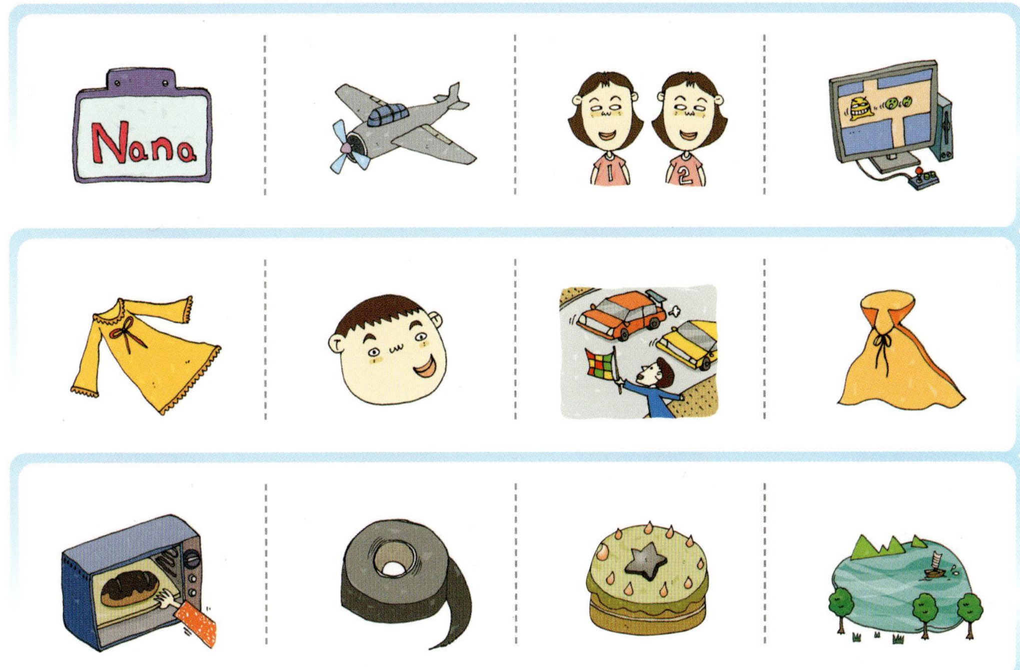

H Look and Write.

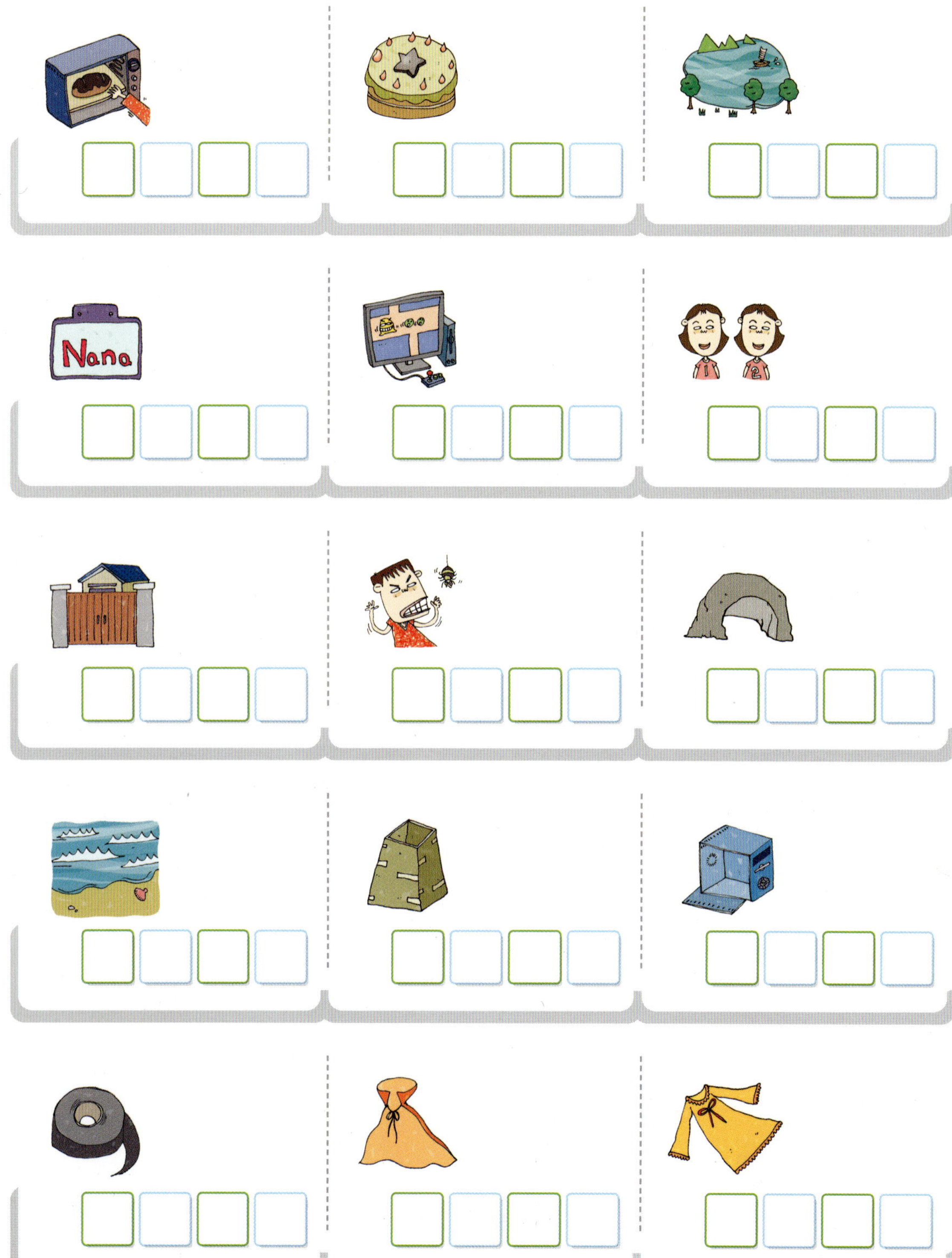

Unit 7 Long Vowel i

A Circle and Write.

h / b + ike / ide

k / v + ike / ite

r / l + ide / ive

f / t + ipe / ive

f / p + ine / ile

B Check the right pictures.

pile

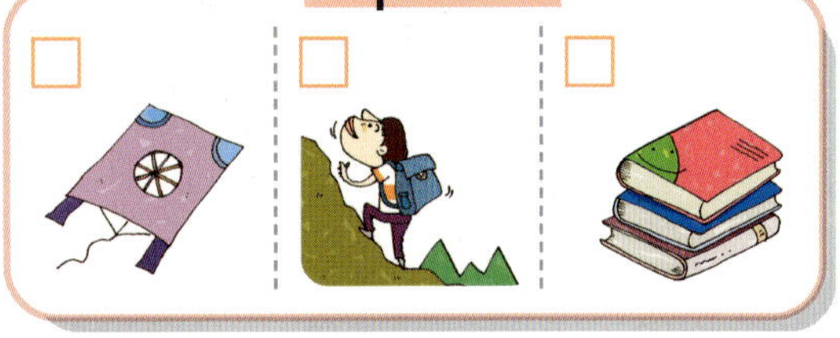

like

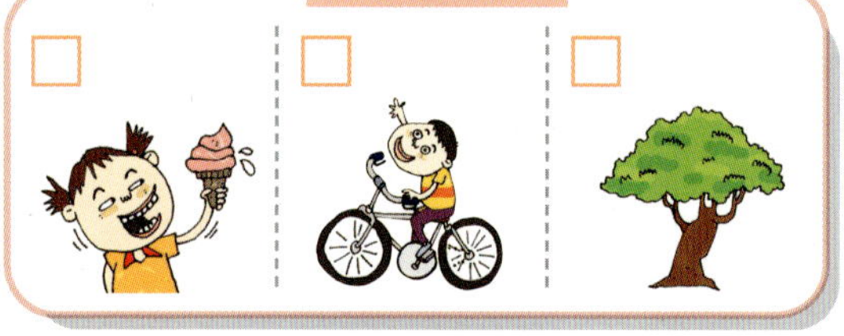

dive

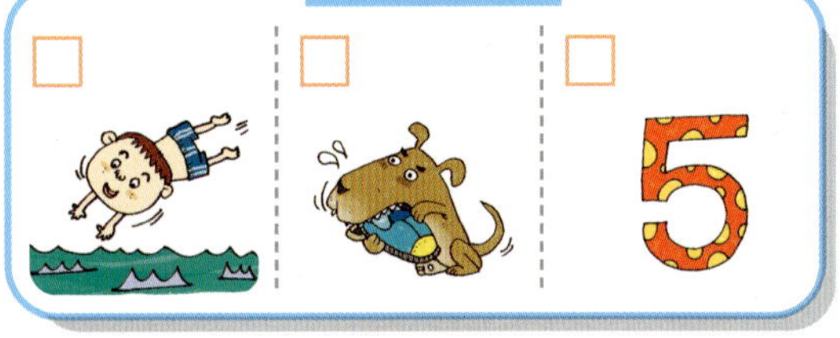

side

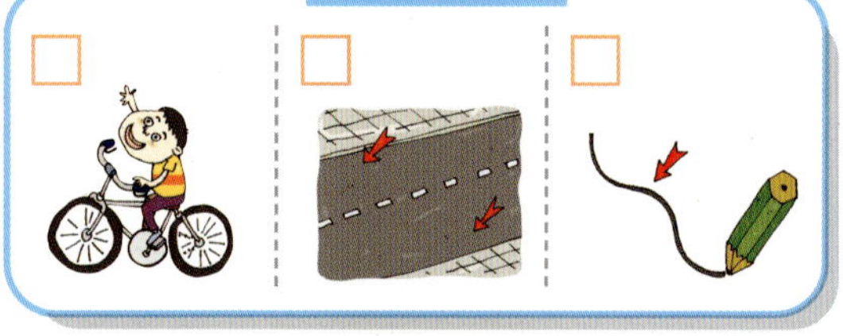

wipe

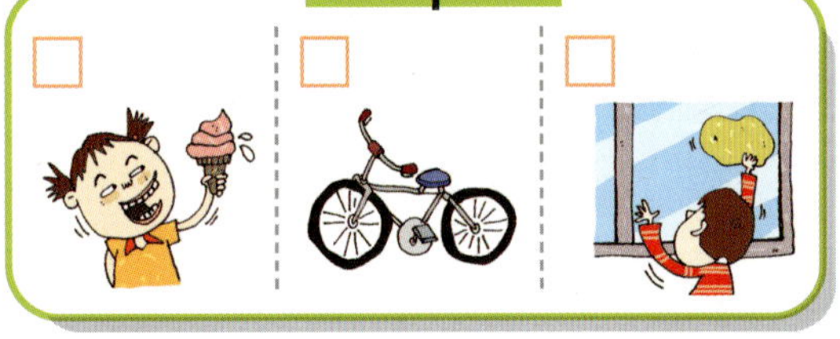

smile

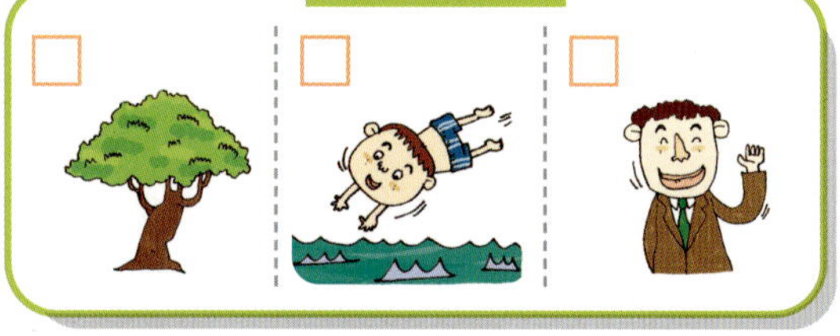

C Match the words with the pictures.

hike

line

bite

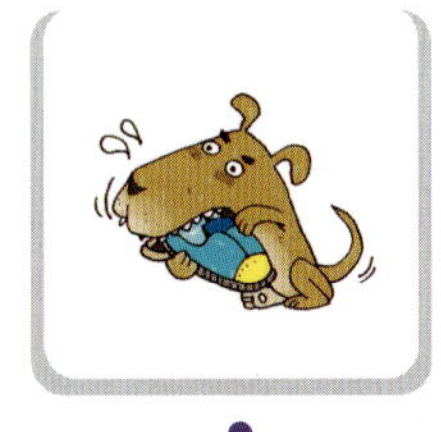

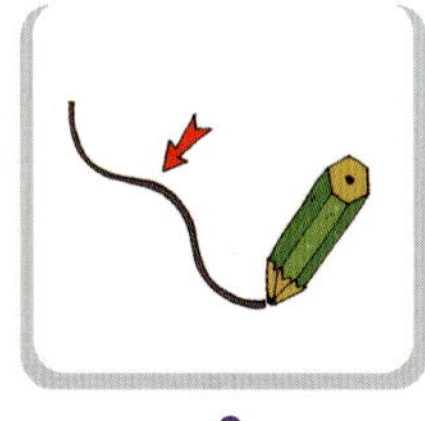

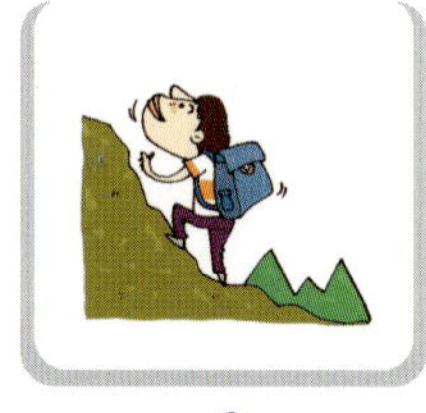

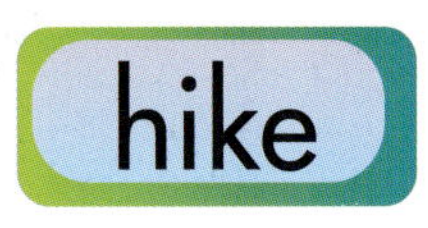

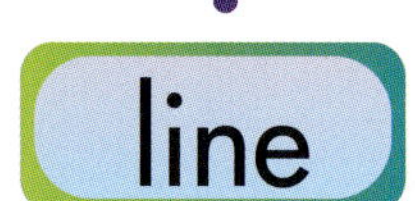

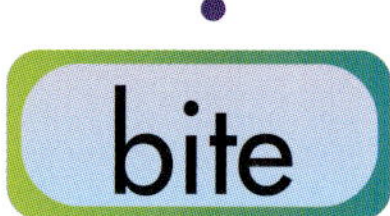

D   Write the correct letters.

 l

 d

 b

 h

 w

 p

 r

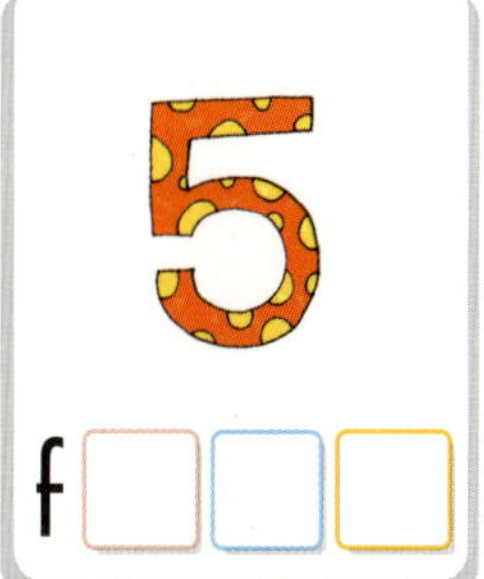 f

E   Match and Color.

pine

kite

bike

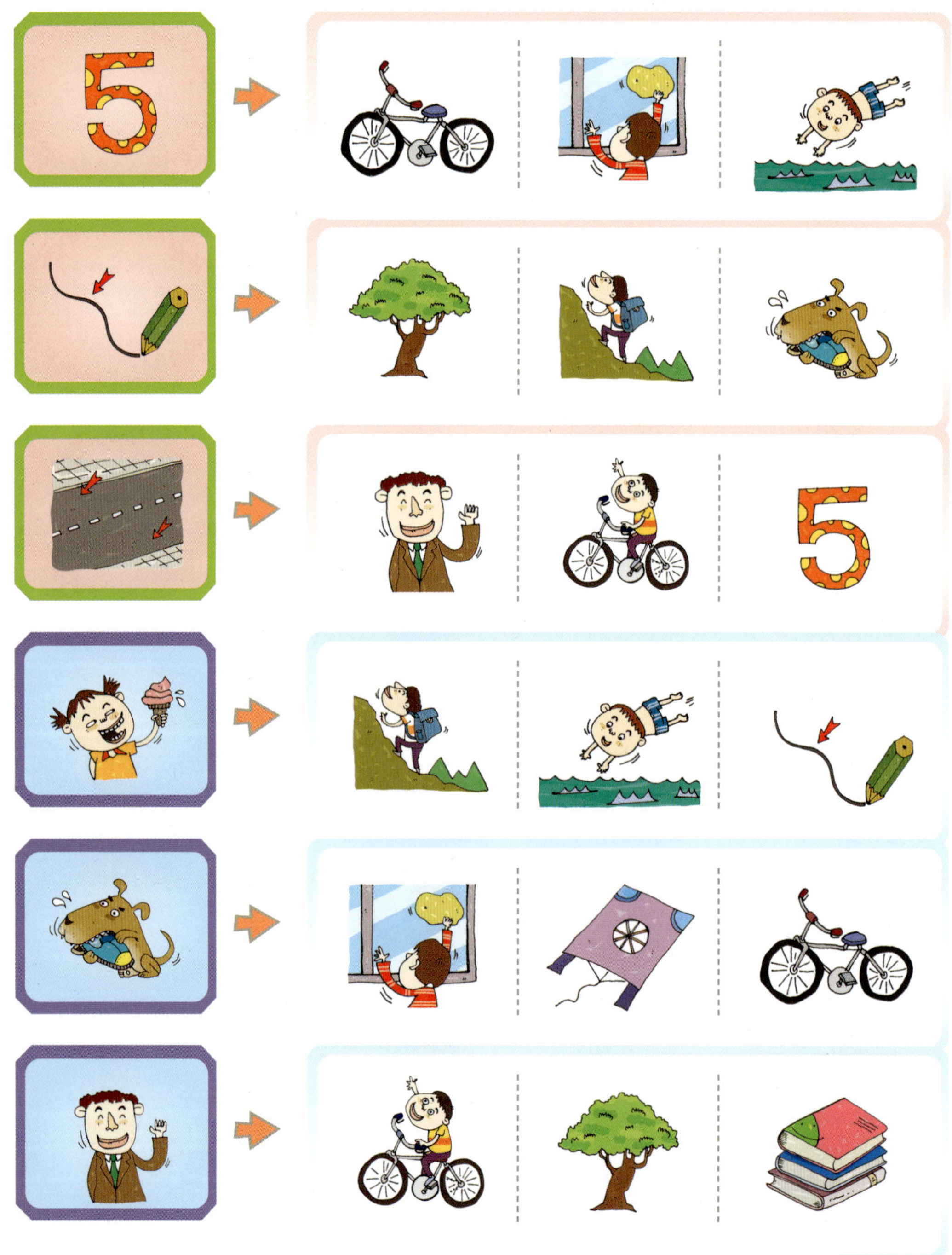

H Look and Write.

Unit 8 Long Vowel O

A Circle and Write.

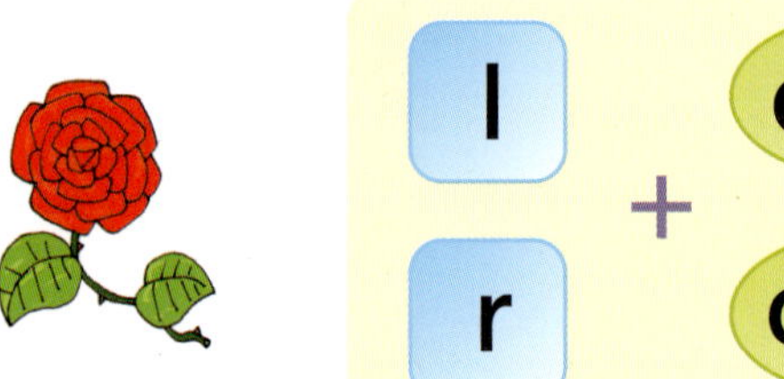

l	+	ose
r		obe

h	+	ote
k		ope

n	+	ole
v		ote

h	+	one
c		ome

m	+	ole
l		ope

B Check the right pictures.

home

hole

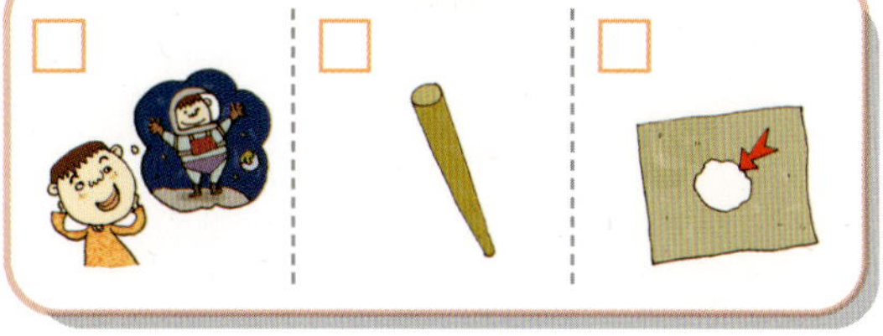

nose

rope

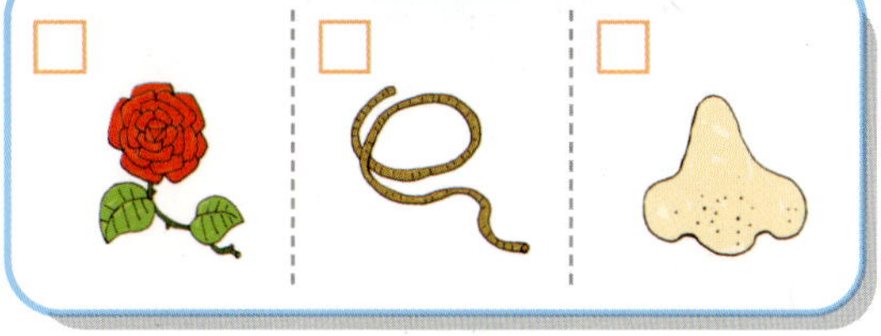

vote

bone

C Match the words with the pictures.

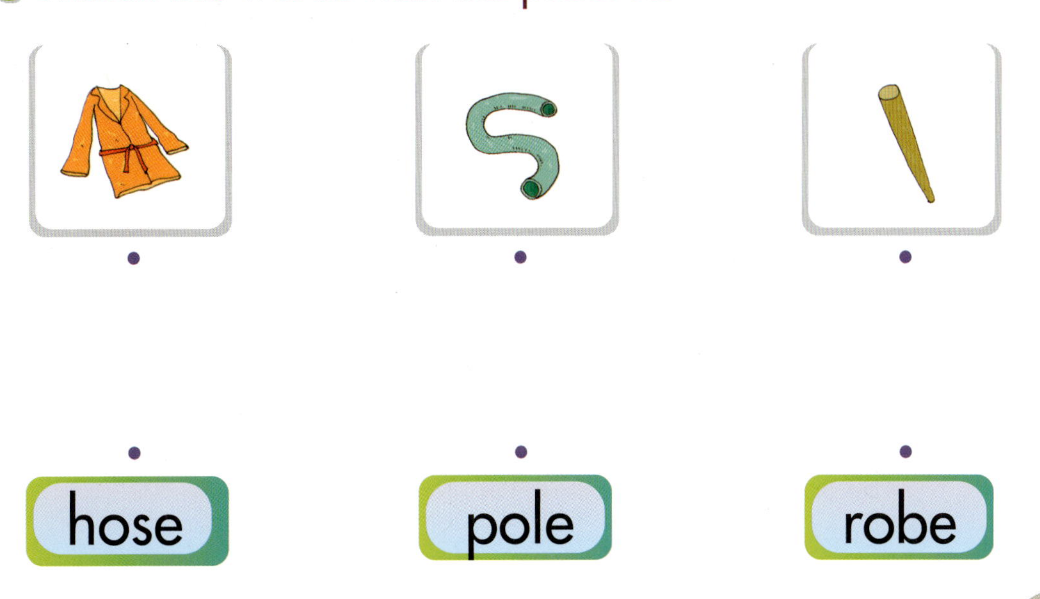

chose

pole

robe

 Write the correct letters.

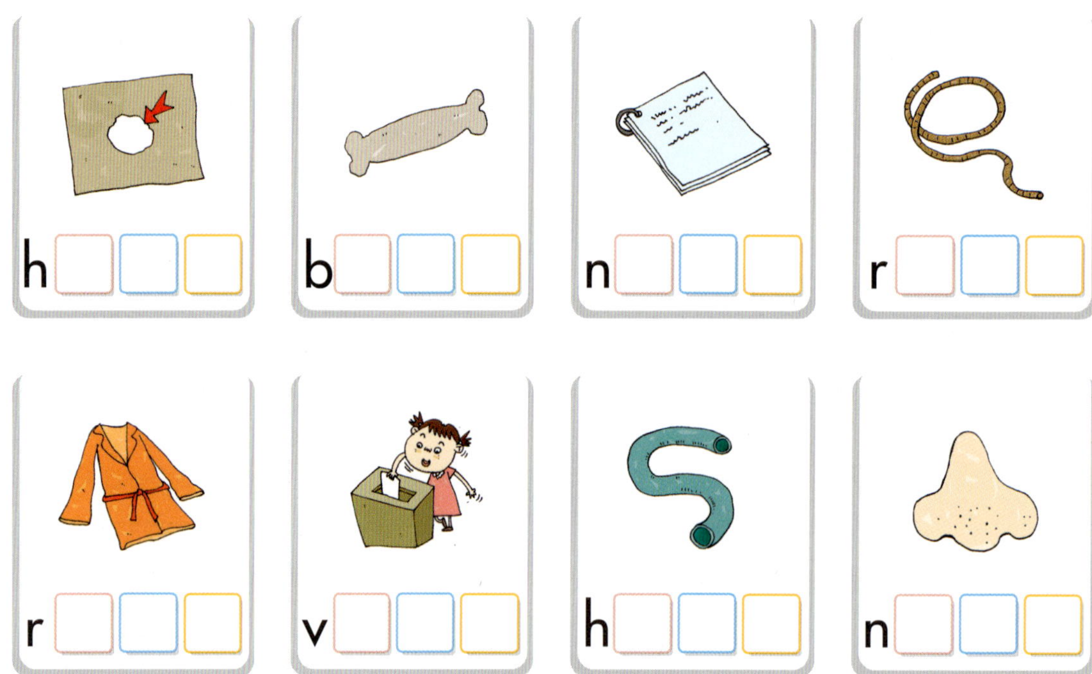

h □ □ □   b □ □ □   n □ □ □   r □ □ □

r □ □ □   v □ □ □   h □ □ □   n □ □ □

E Match and Color.

F Circle the pictures that rhyme with the first pictures.

G Circle the pictures that rhyme is Not same.

 Look and Write.

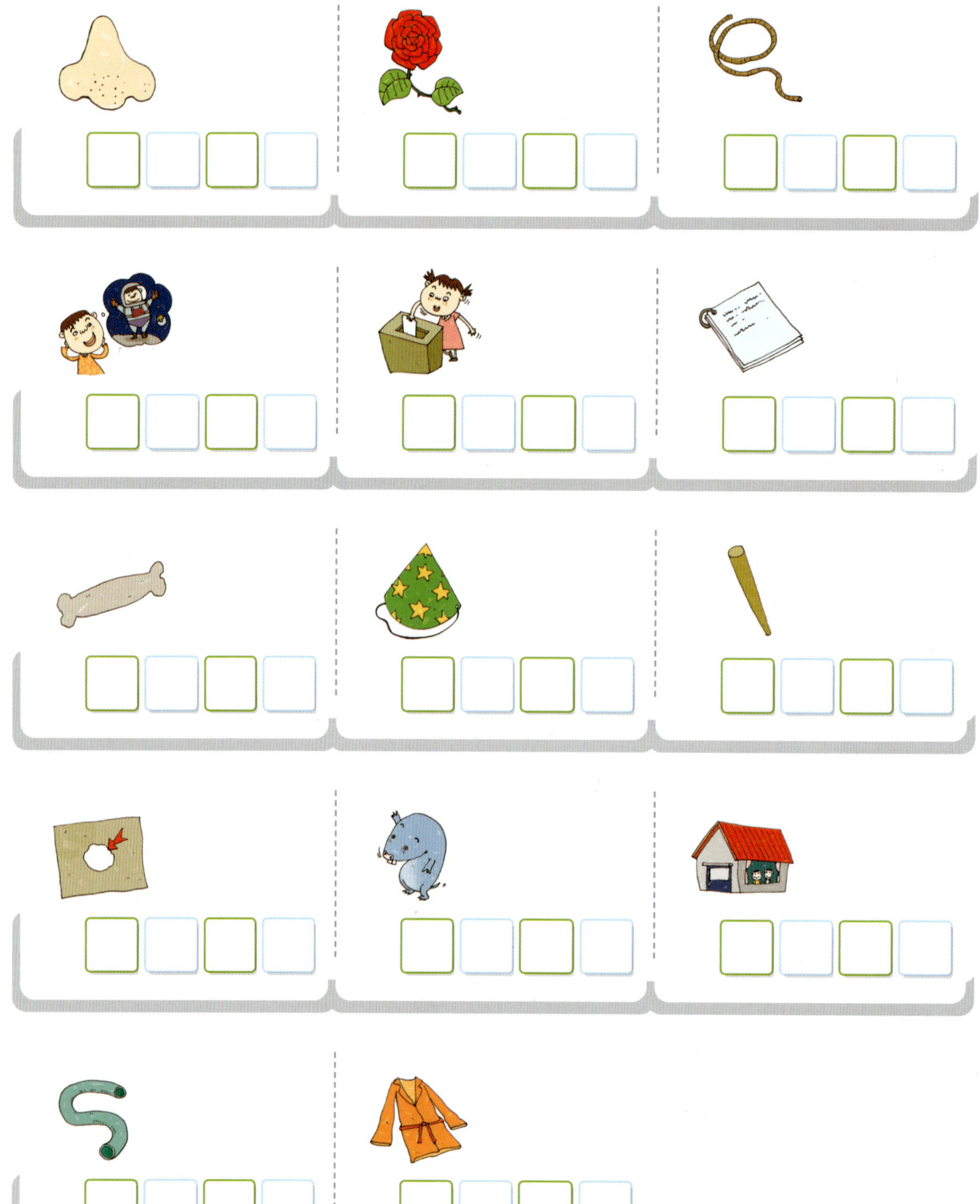

A Circle and Write.

d | t + ube | ute →

b | d + ude | une →

m | n + ube | ule →

k | f + use | une →

c | v + uke | ute →

B Check the right pictures.

huge

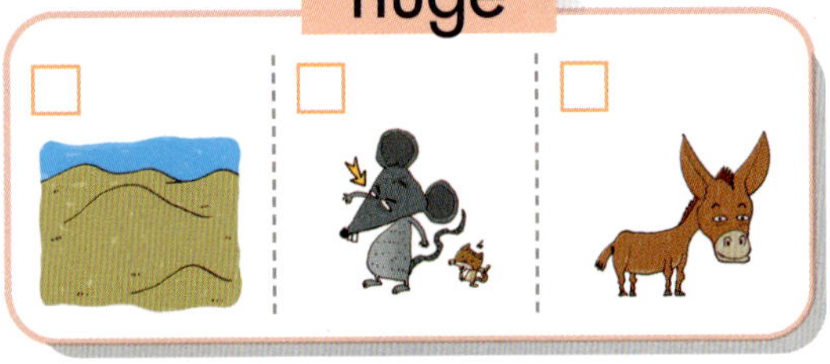

rude

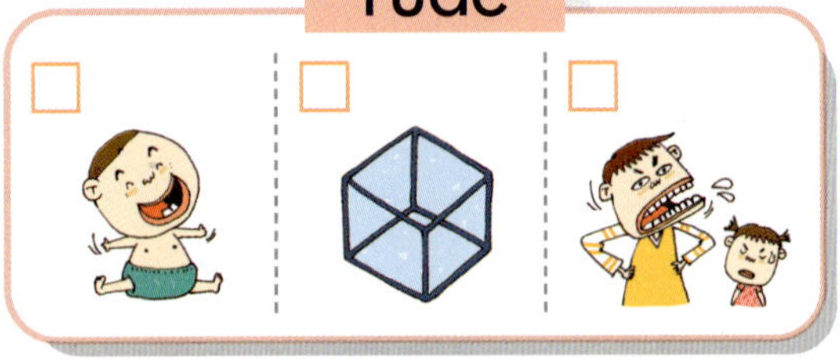

June

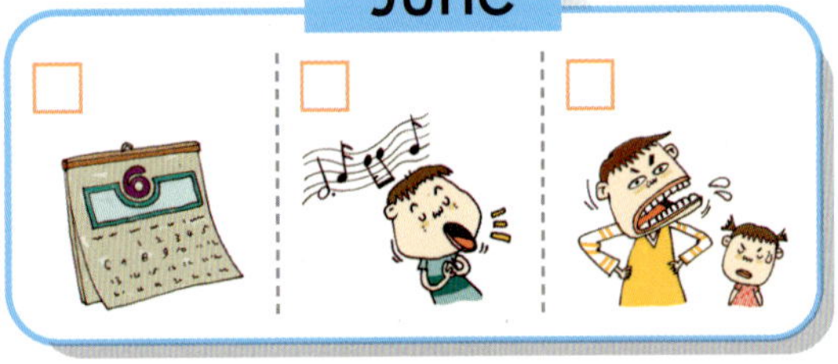

duke

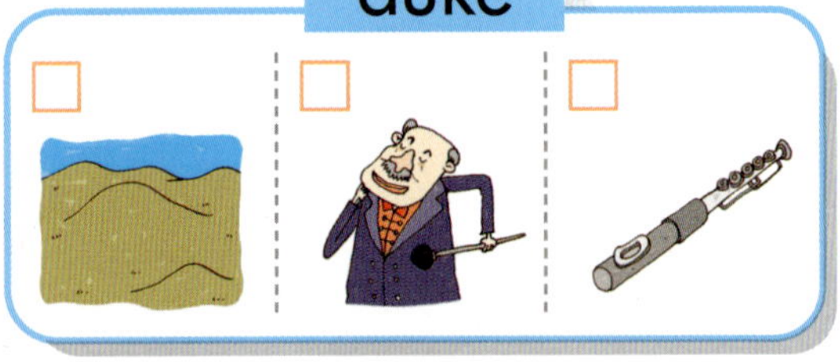

tube

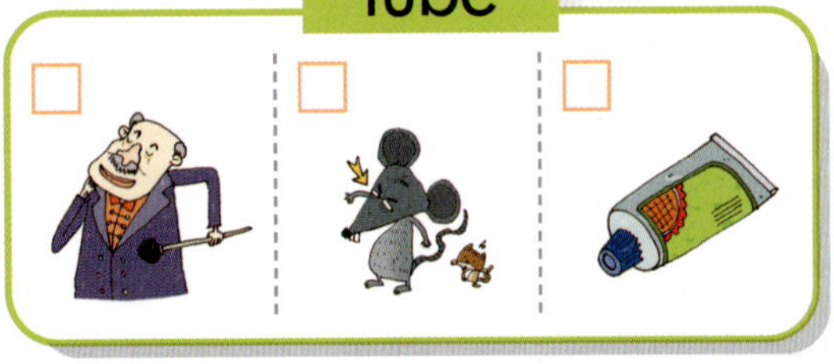

fuse

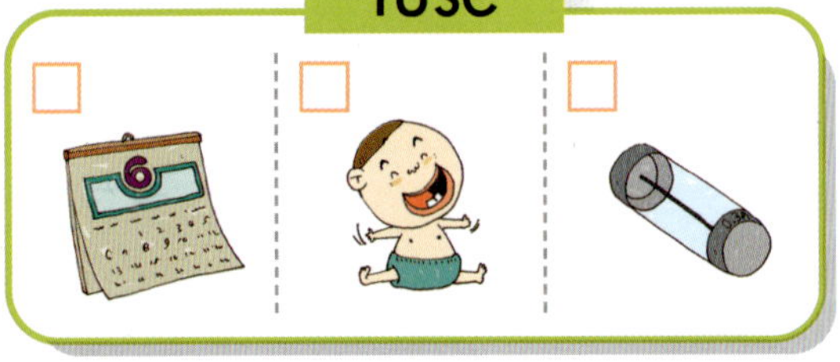

C Match the words with the pictures.

tune   flute   cube

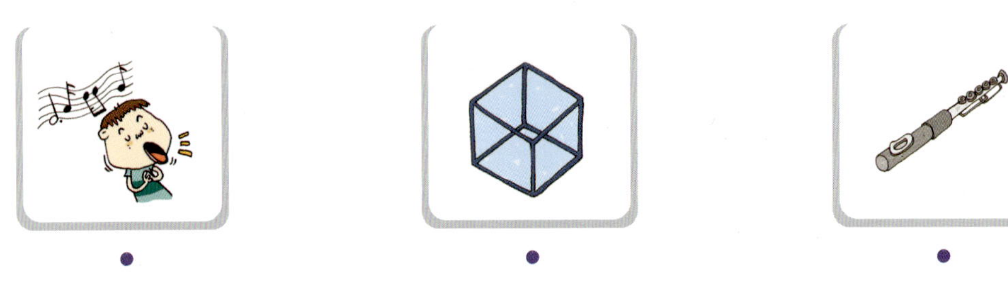

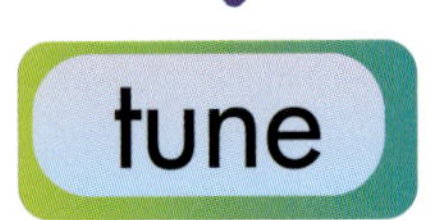

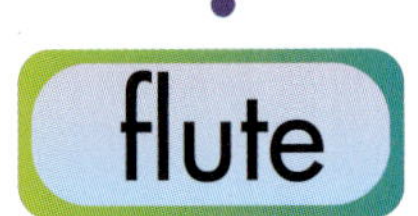

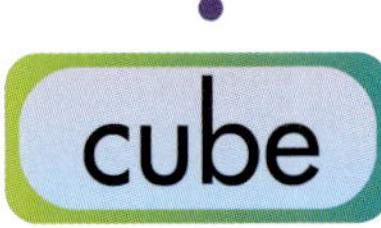

D Write the correct letters.

 J □ □ □

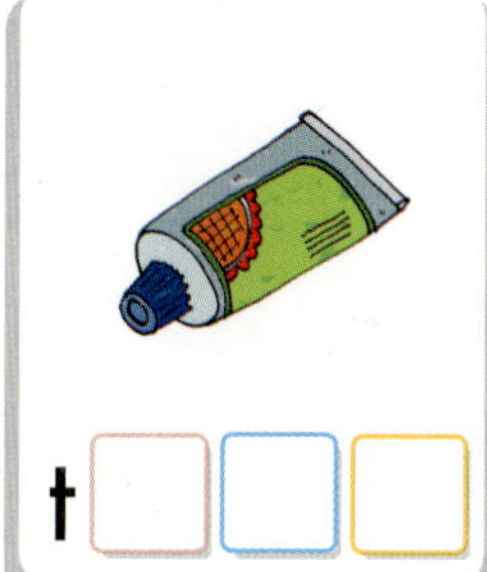 t □ □ □

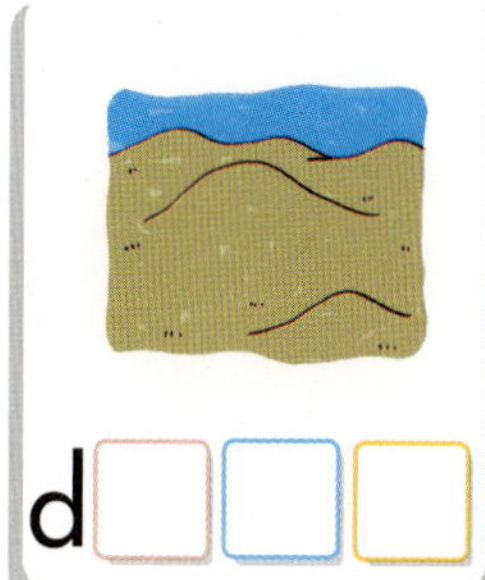 d □ □ □

 m □ □ □

 h □ □ □

 t □ □ □

 r □ □ □

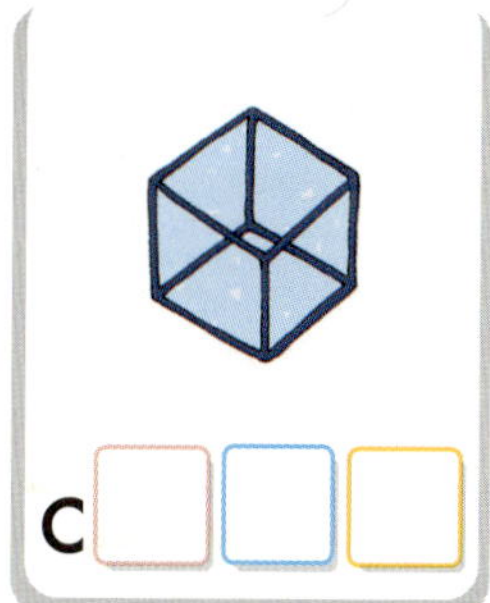 c □ □ □

E Match and Color.

duke   cute   flute

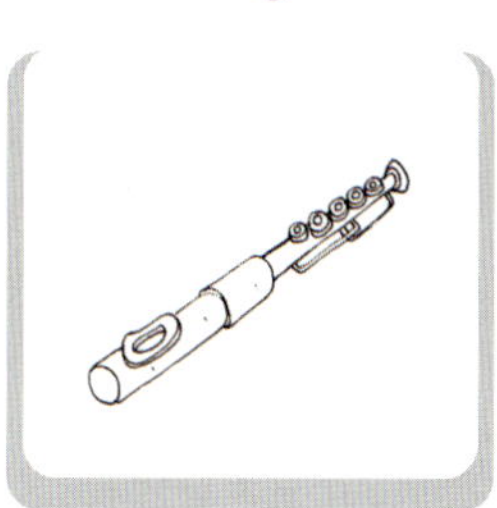  

F Circle the pictures that rhyme with the first pictures.

G Circle the pictures that rhyme is Not same.

H Look and Write.

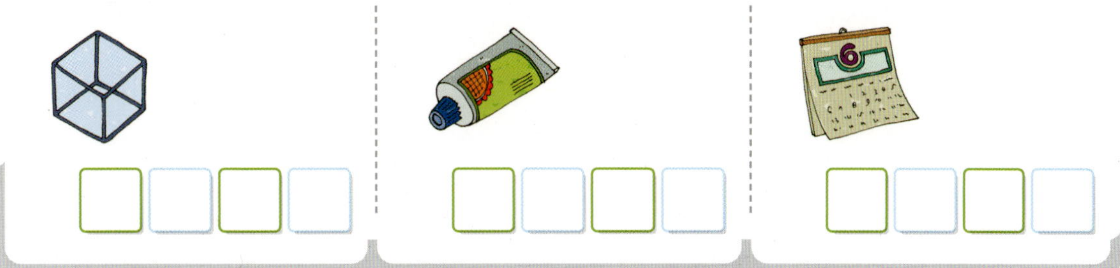

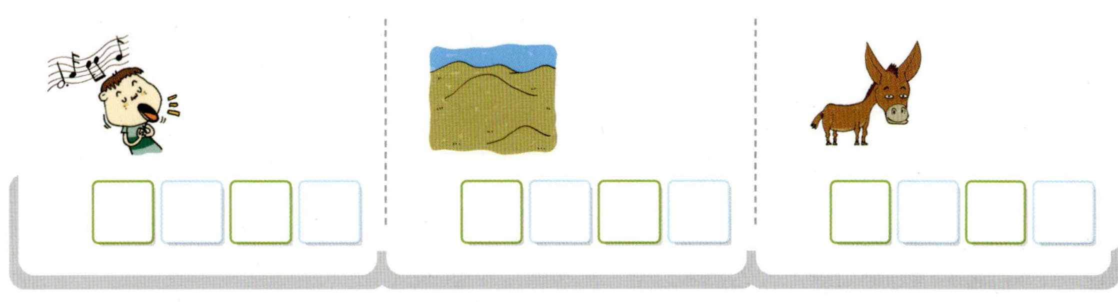

A Circle the pictures with the match sounds.

long **a** sound

  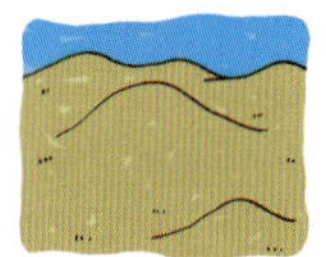 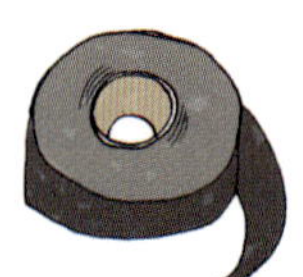

long **i** sound

long **o** sound

long **u** sound

B Look and Match.

-ake
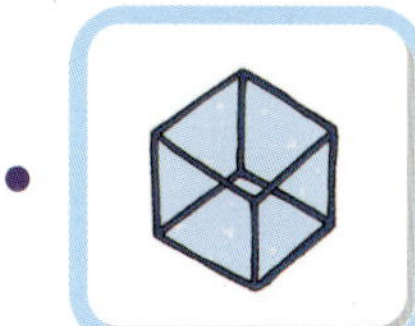

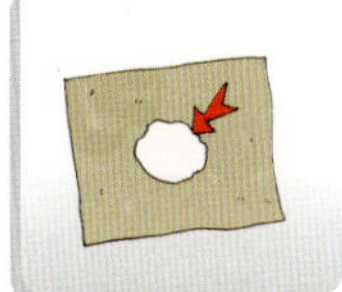

-ube

-ole

-ive

-ote

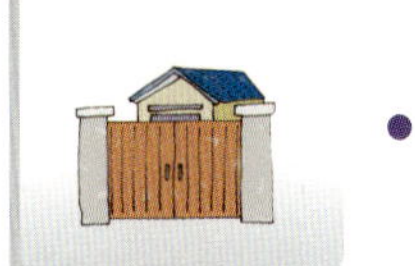

-ate

plane

duke

wipe

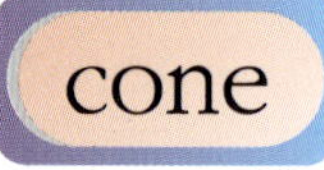
cone

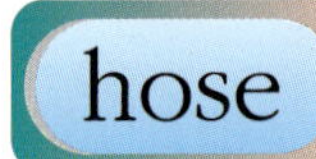
hose

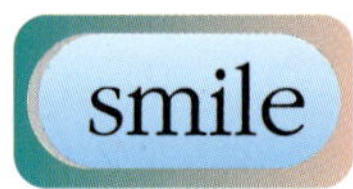
smile

rude

face

D Check the right words.

E Write the correct letters.

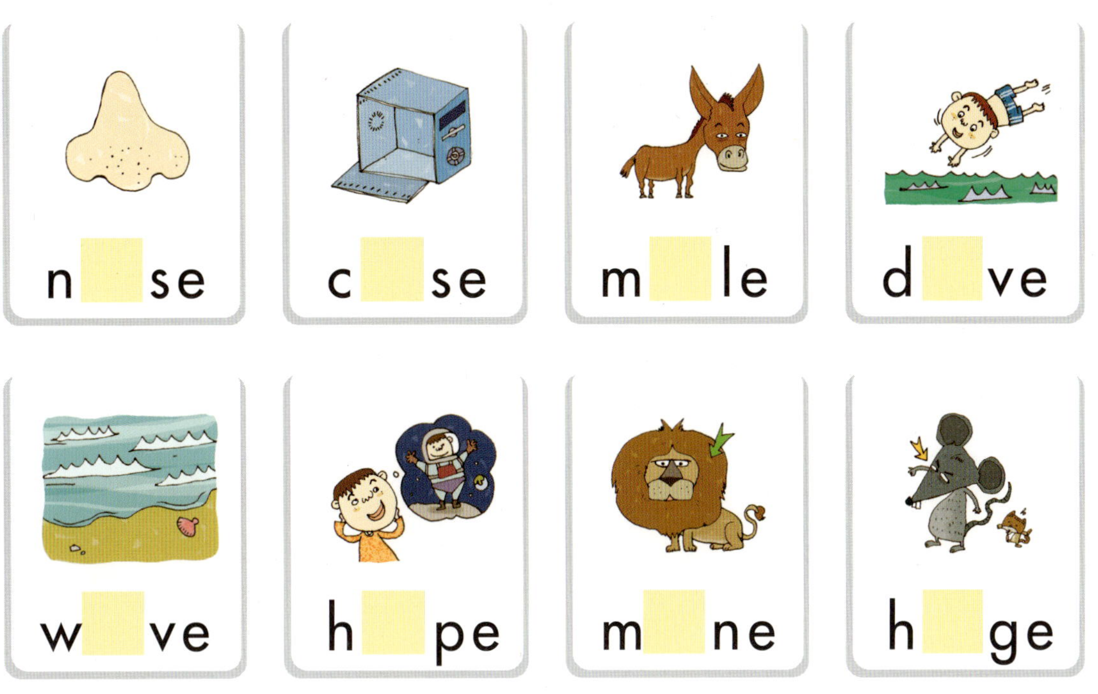

 Look and Write.

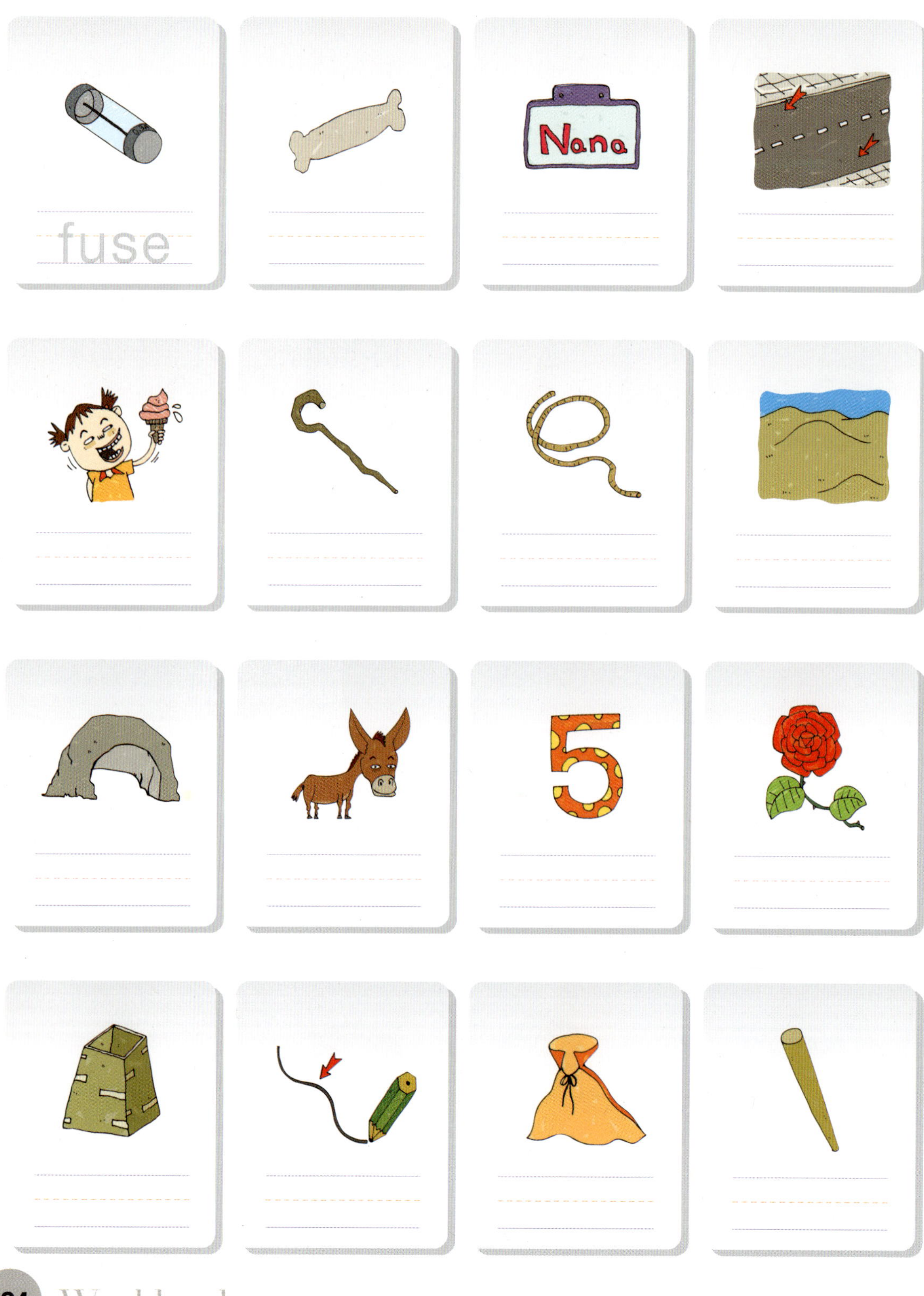

Final Test

A Look and Match the same sounds.

B Read and Check.

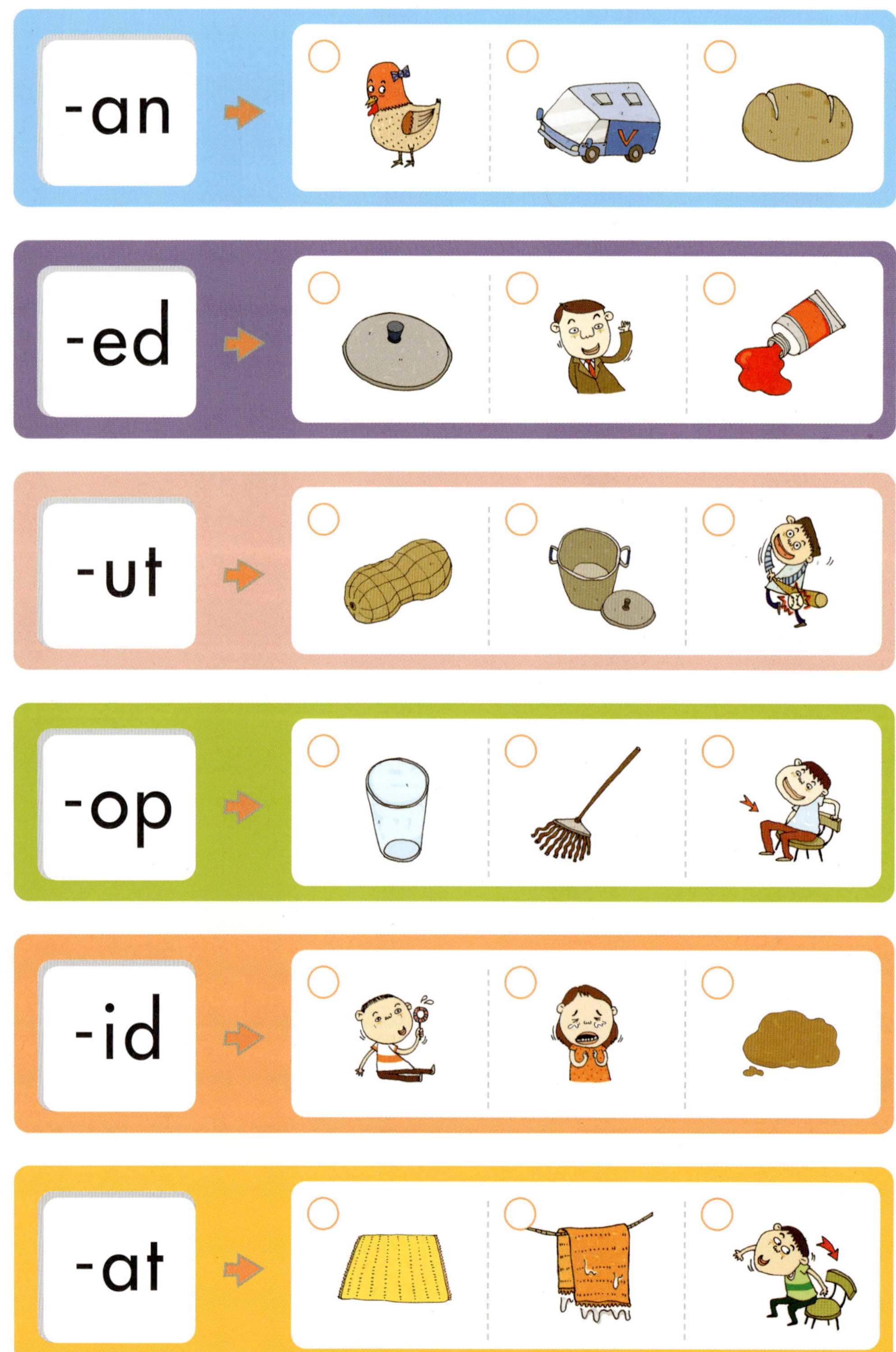

-an
-ed
-ut
-op
-id
-at

C Read and Check.

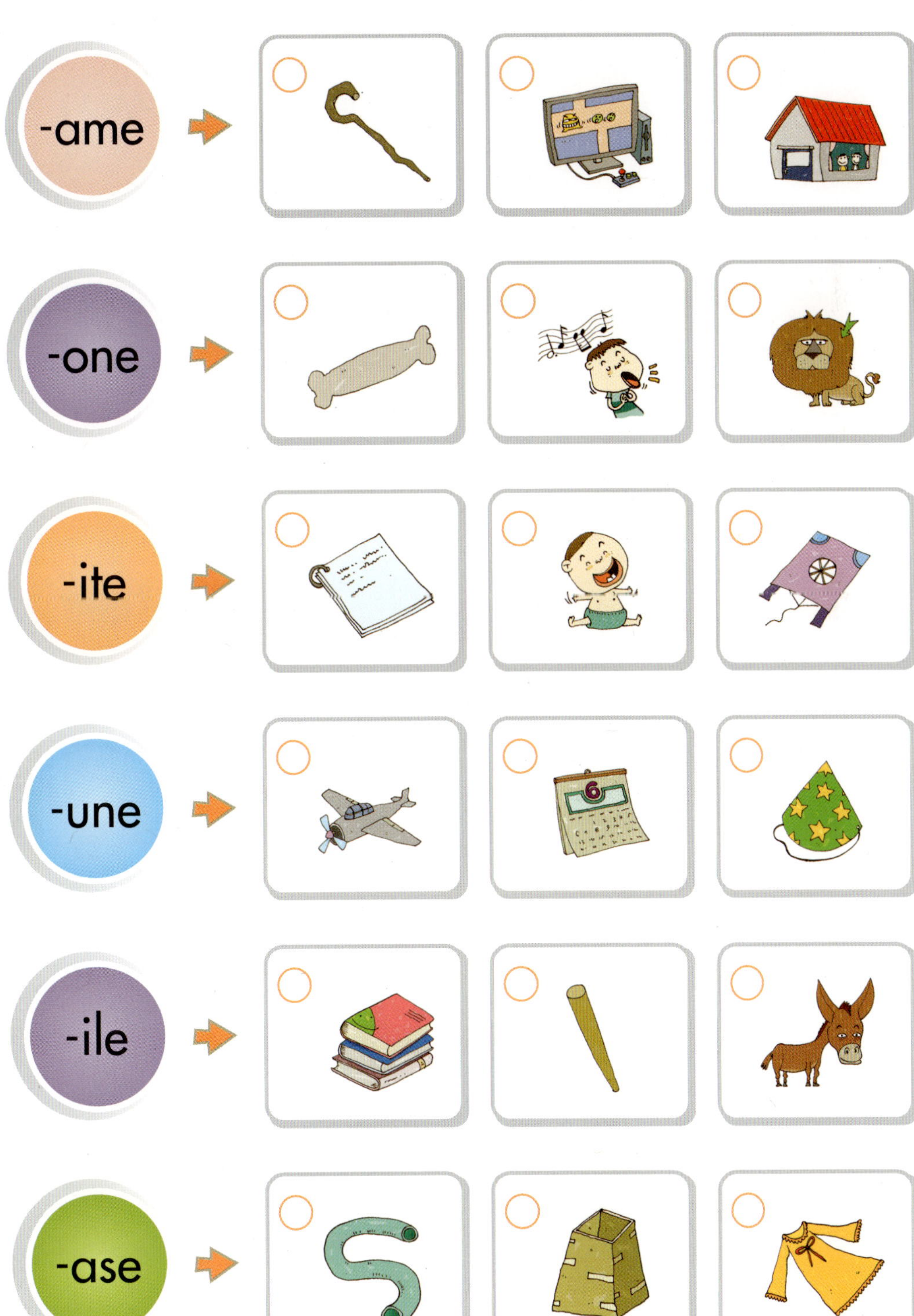

 Write the correct letters.(Short Vowels)

E Write the correct letters. (Long Vowels)

  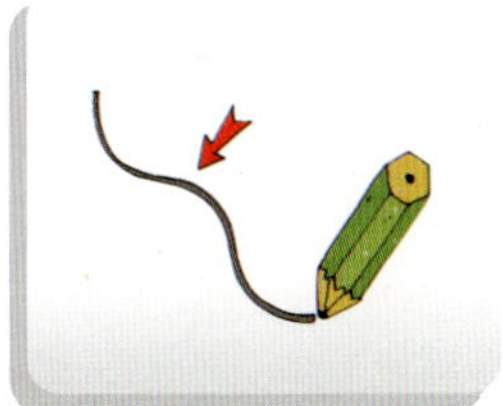 

h 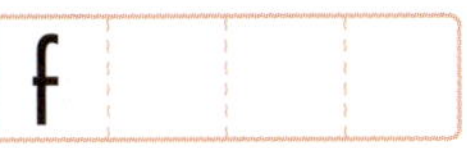 f  l  r

b m d r

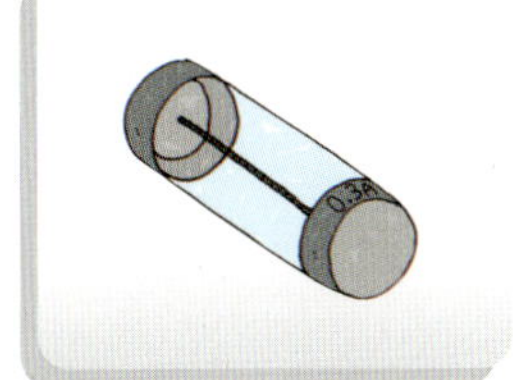   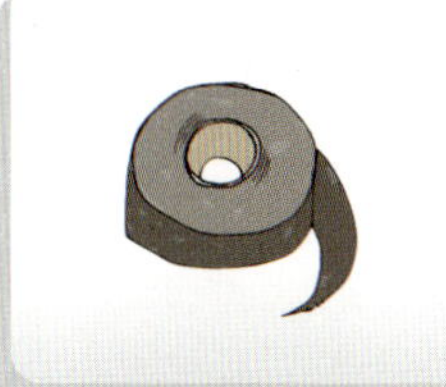

f  b  r t

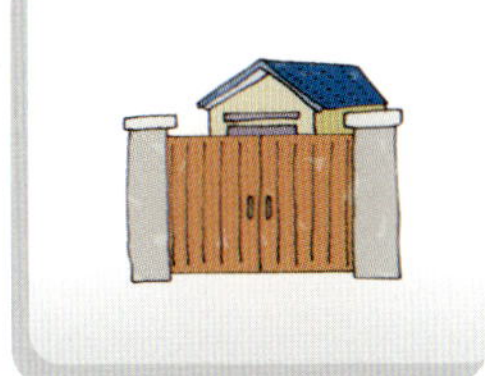   

g 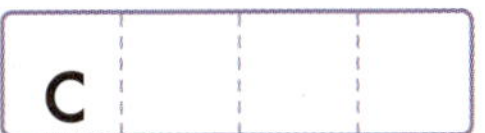 c 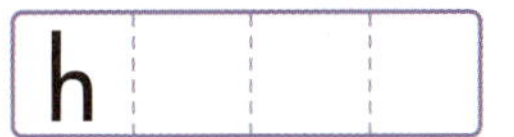 h w

Answer Key

140p

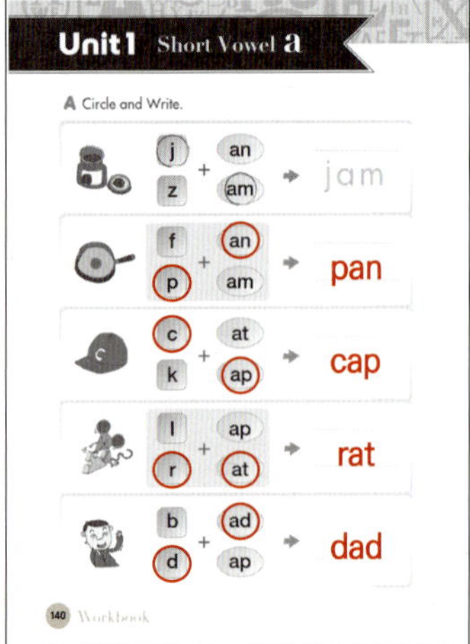

141p

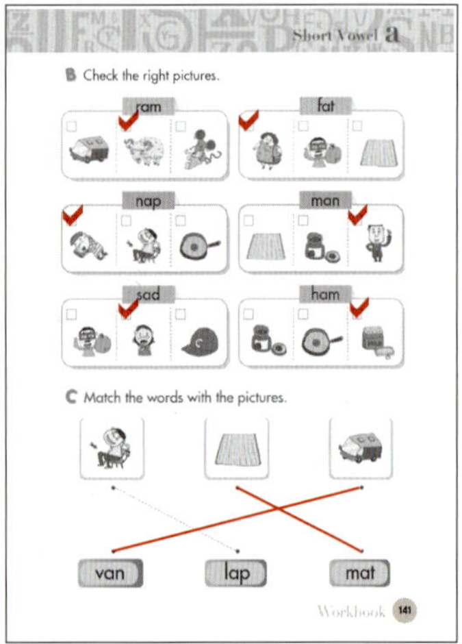

142p

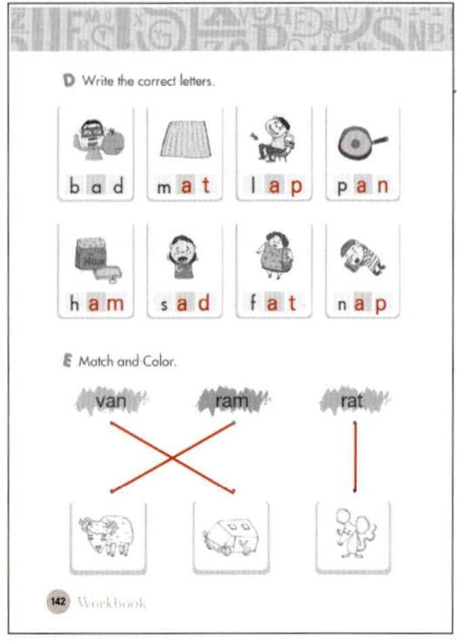

143p

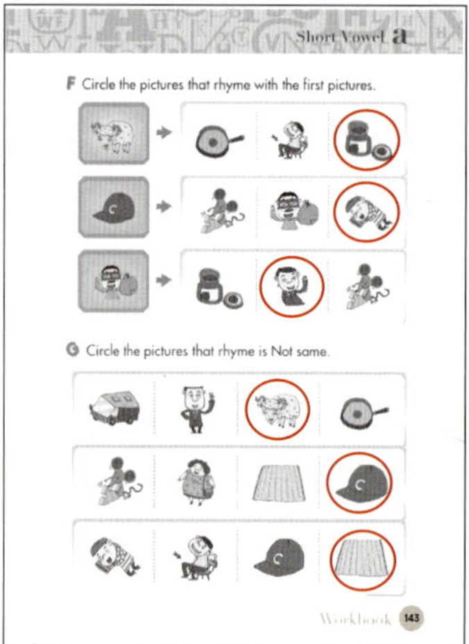

144p

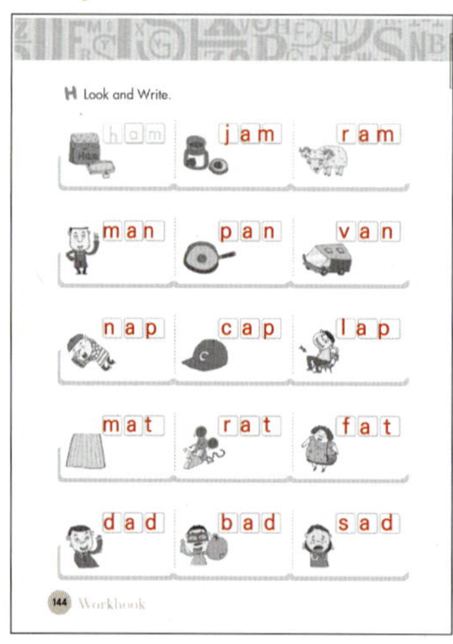

145p

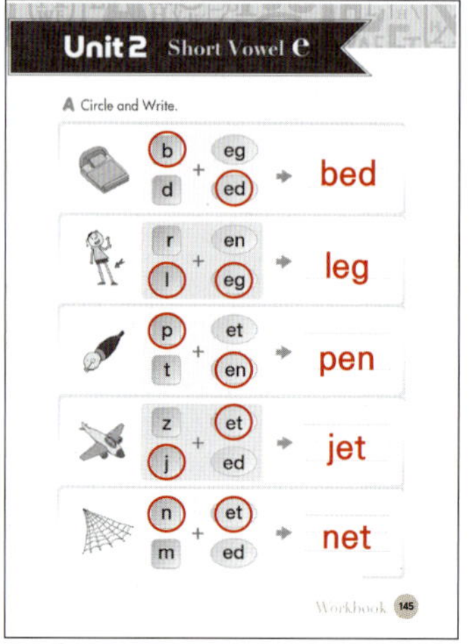

146p

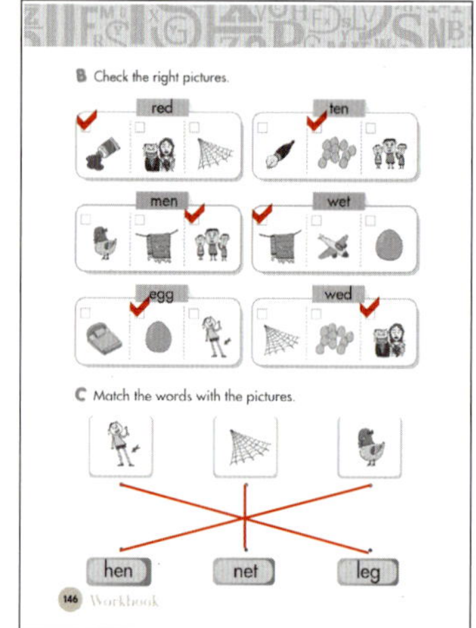

147p

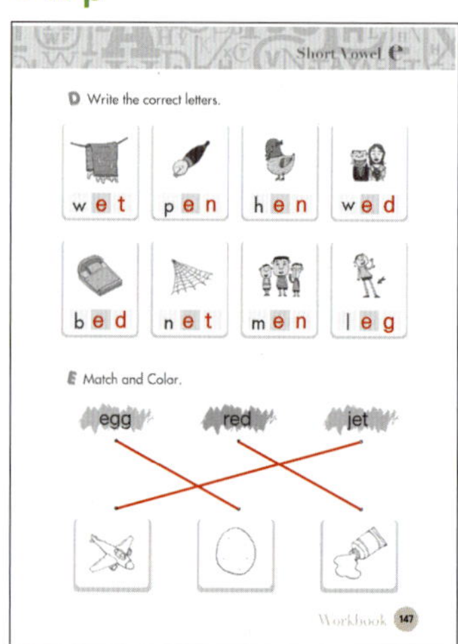

148p

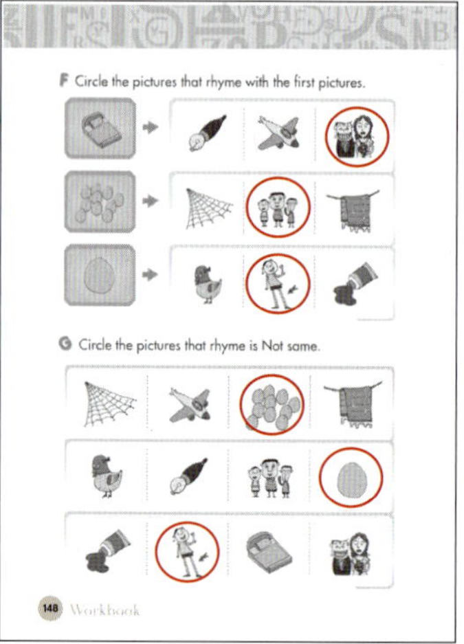

Answer Key

149p

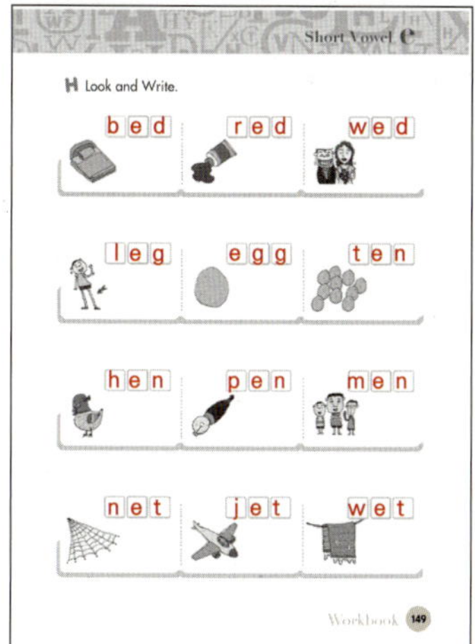

150p

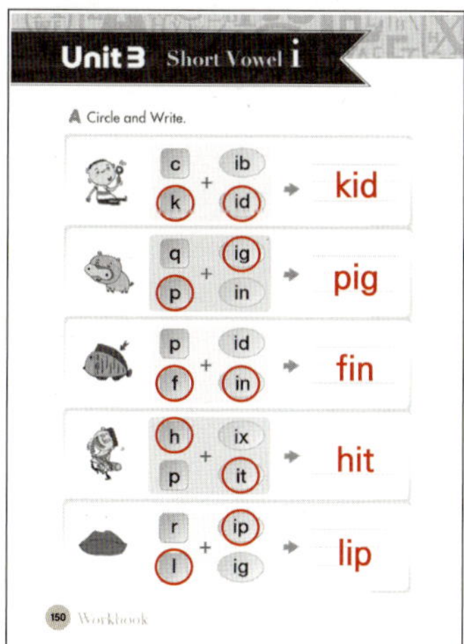

151p

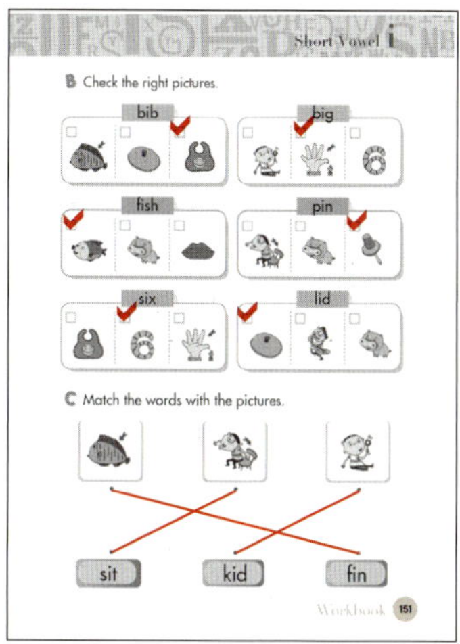

152p

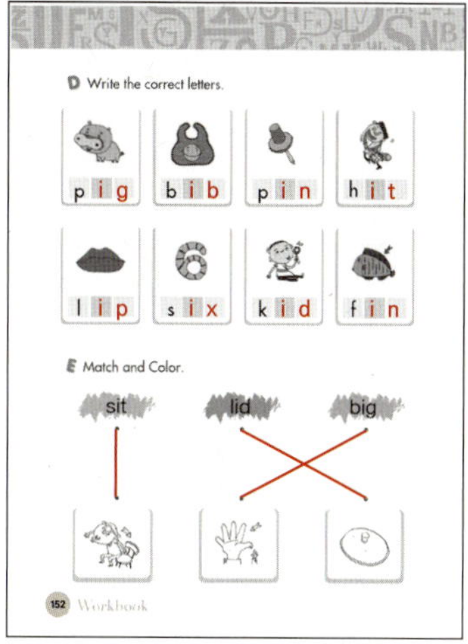

153p

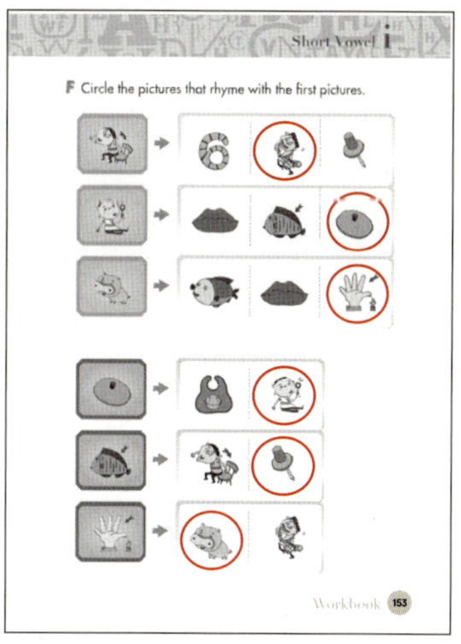

154p

155p

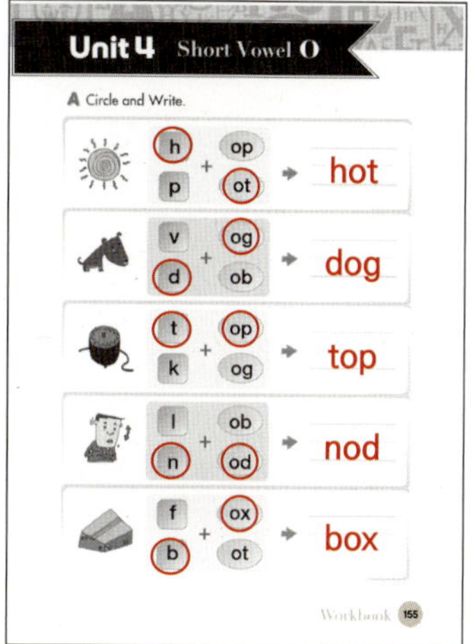

156p

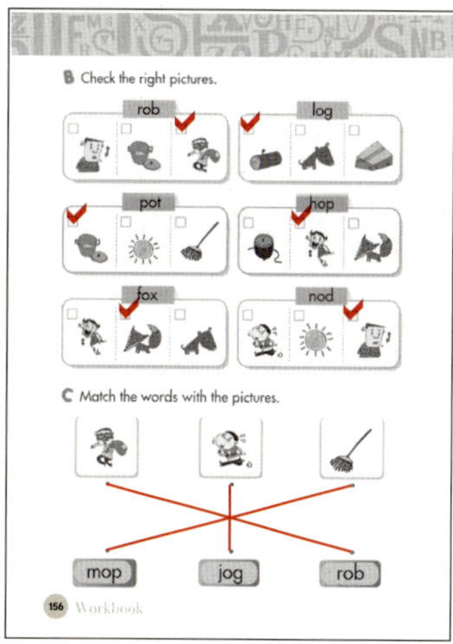

157p

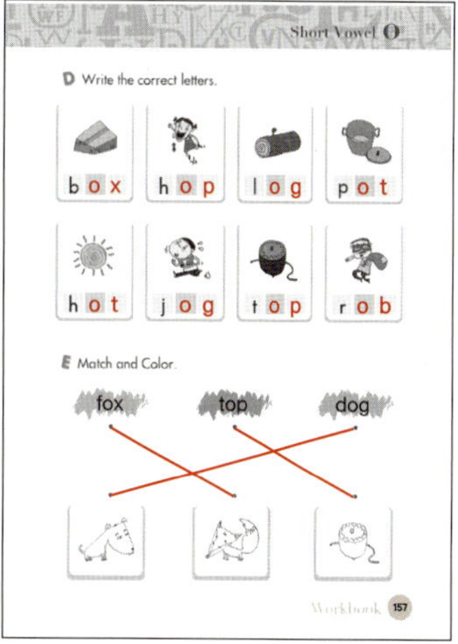

Answer Key

158p

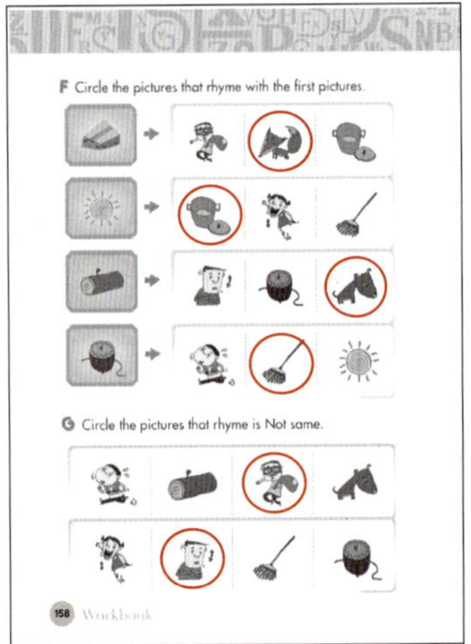

159p

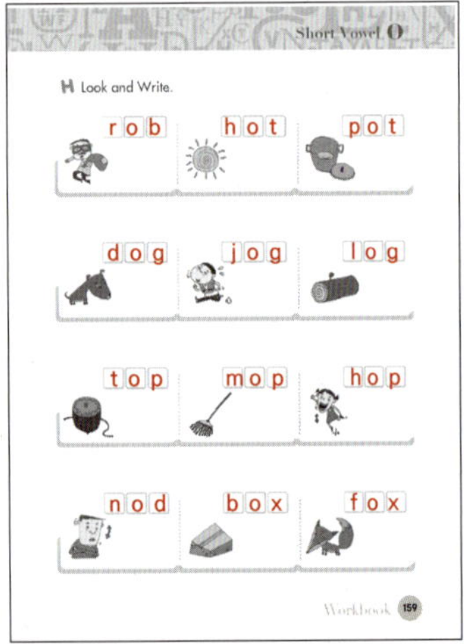

160p

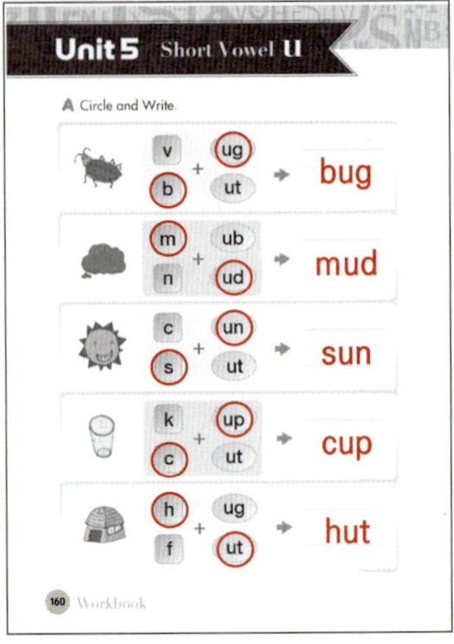

161p

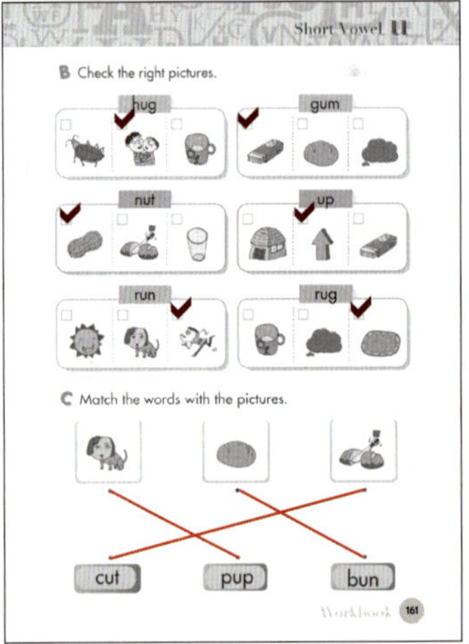

162p

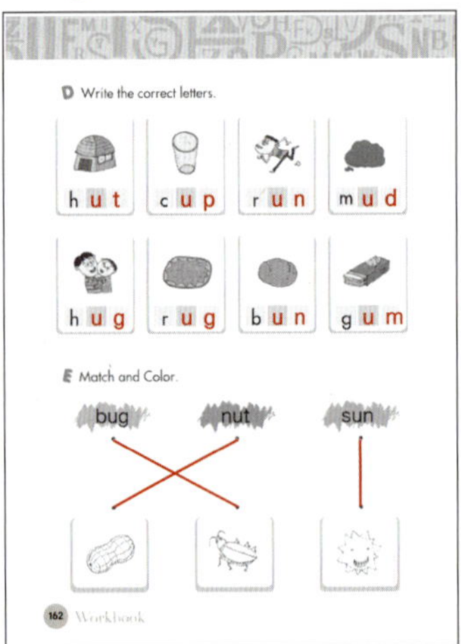

163p

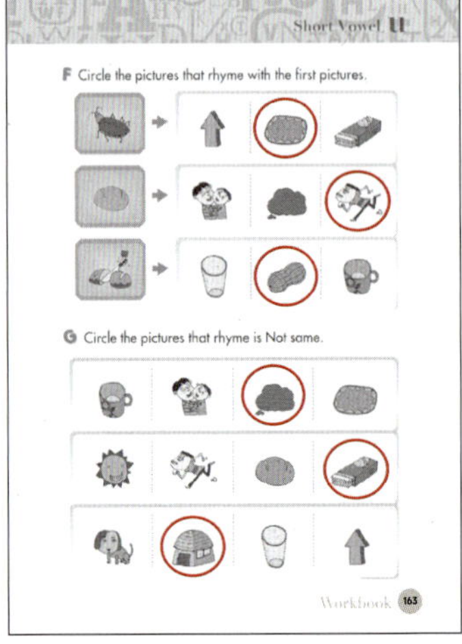

164p

165p

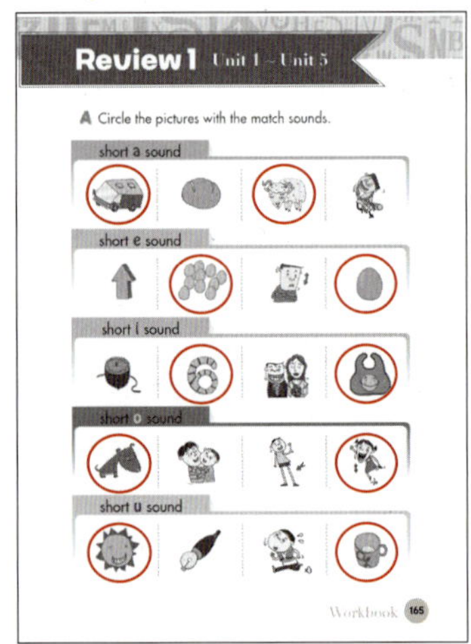

166p

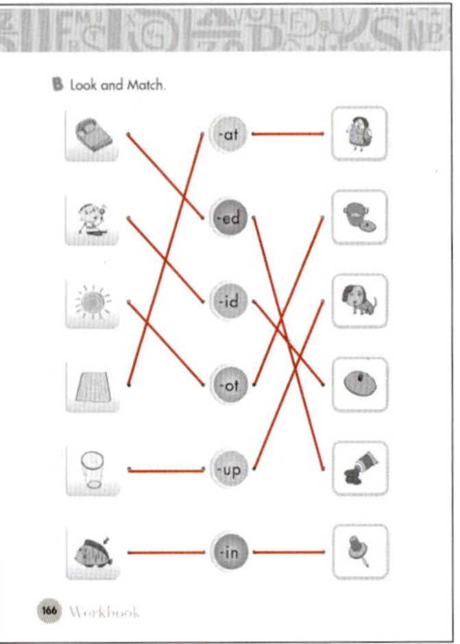

167p

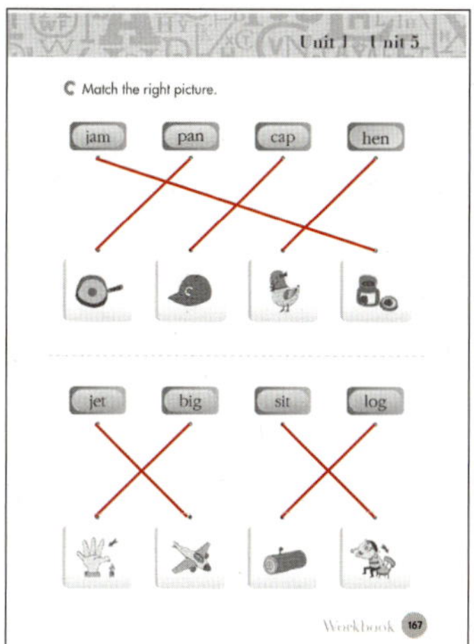

168p

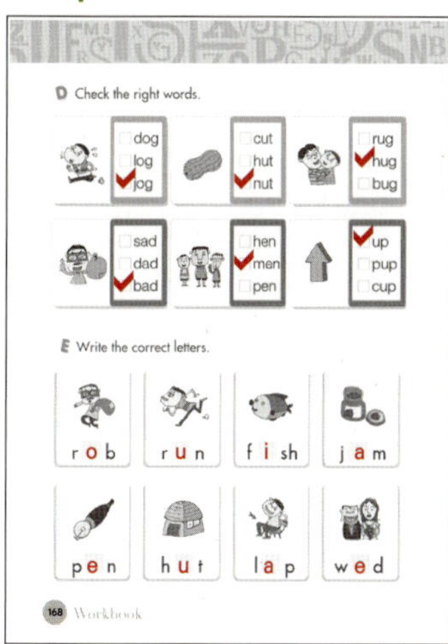

169p

170p

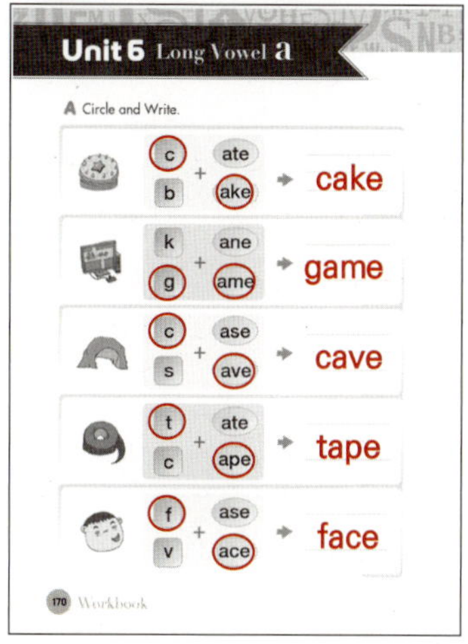

171p

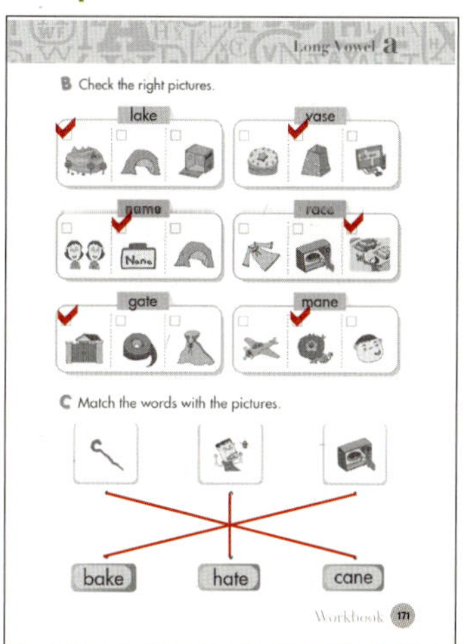

172p

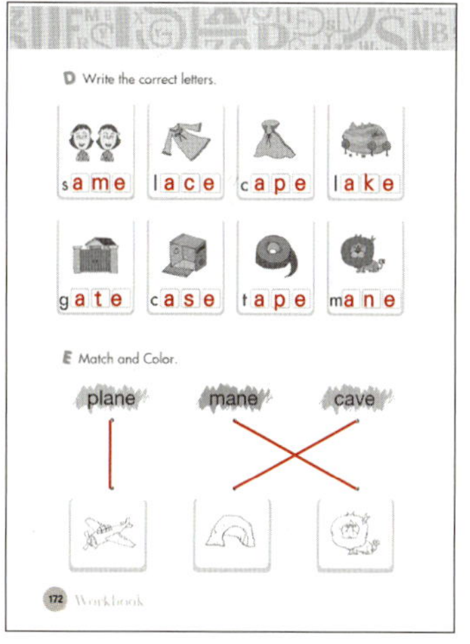

173p

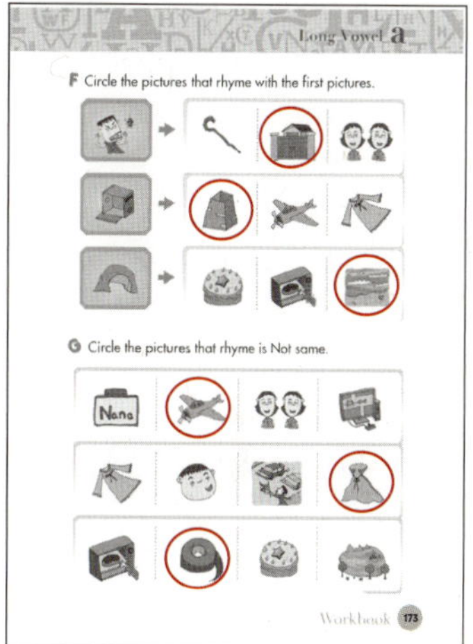

174p

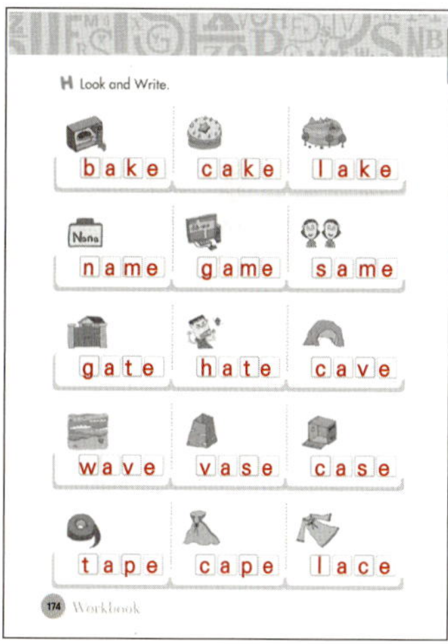

175p

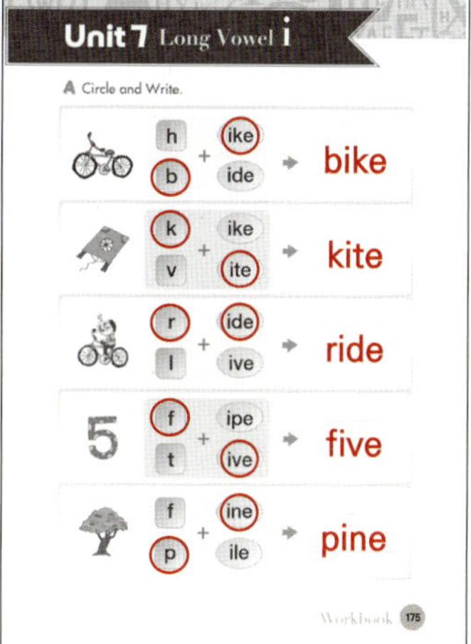

Answer Key

176p

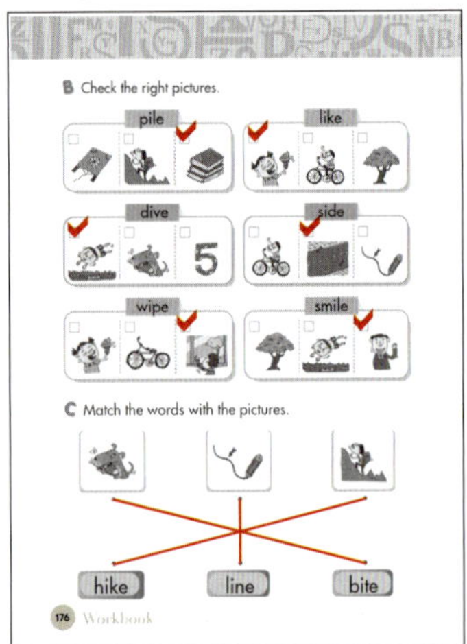

177p

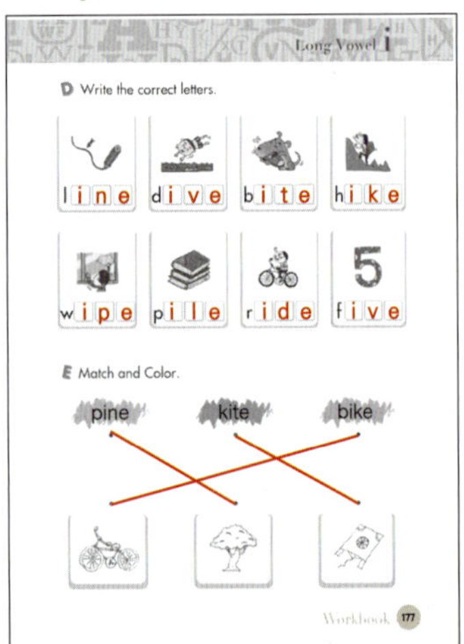

178p

179p

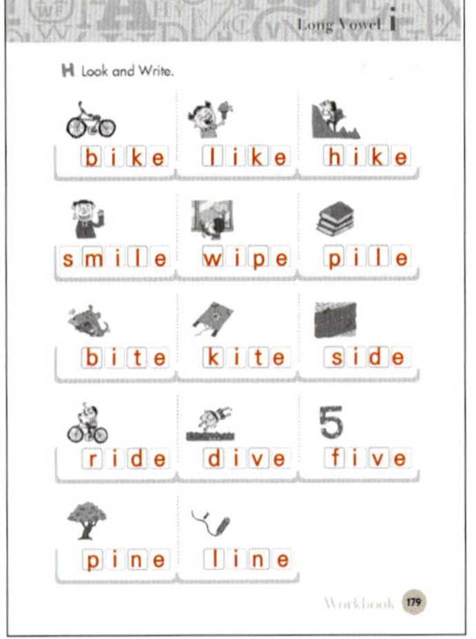

180p

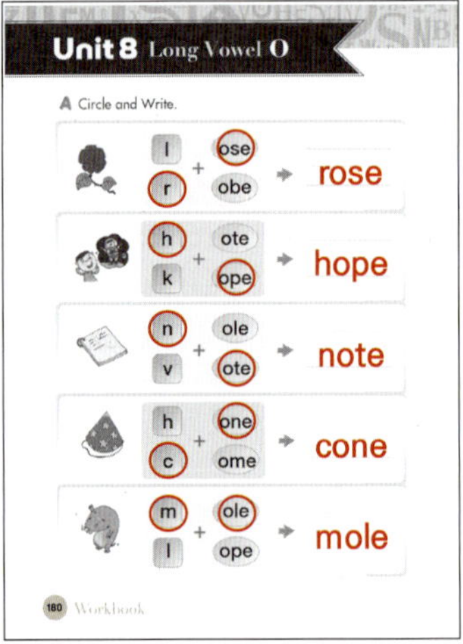

181p

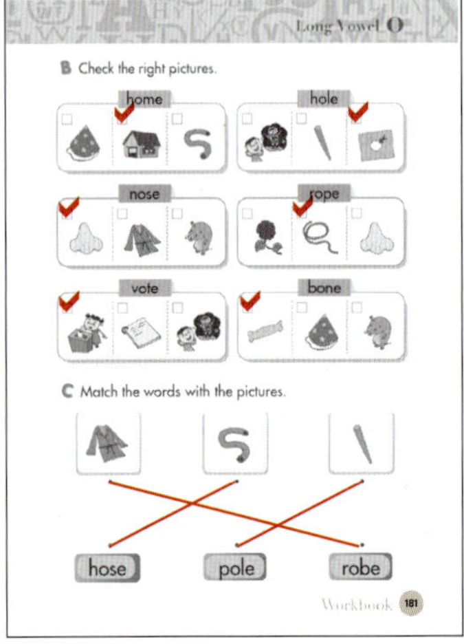

182p

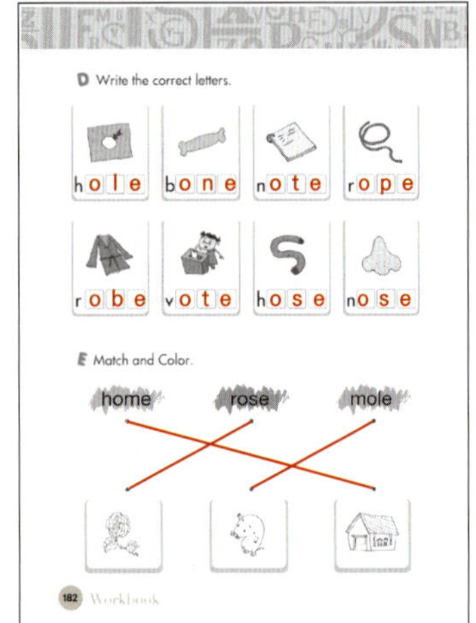

183p

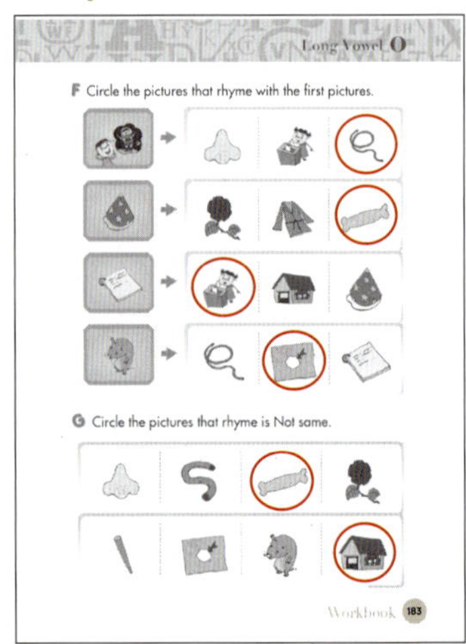

184p

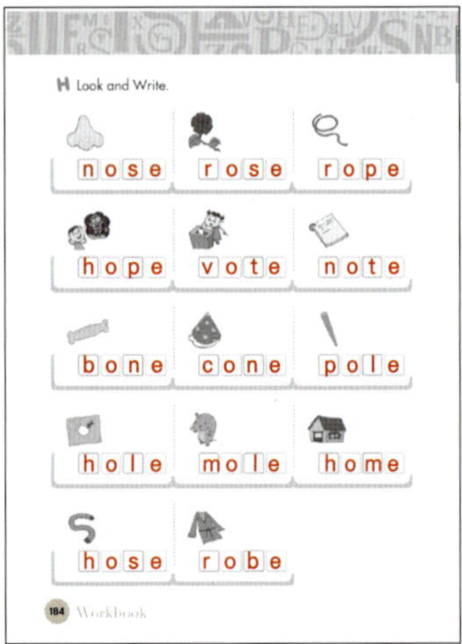

185p

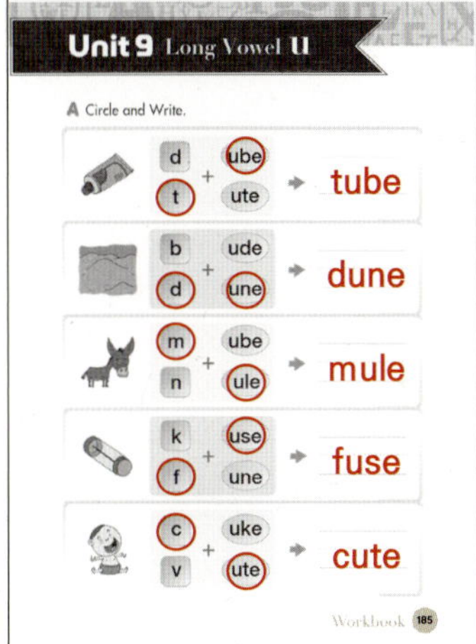

186p

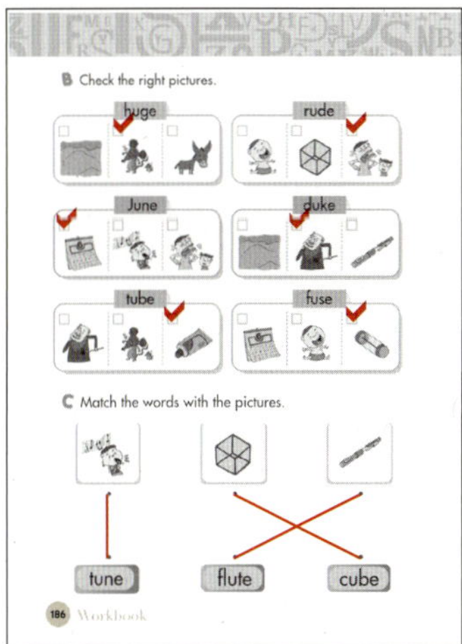

187p

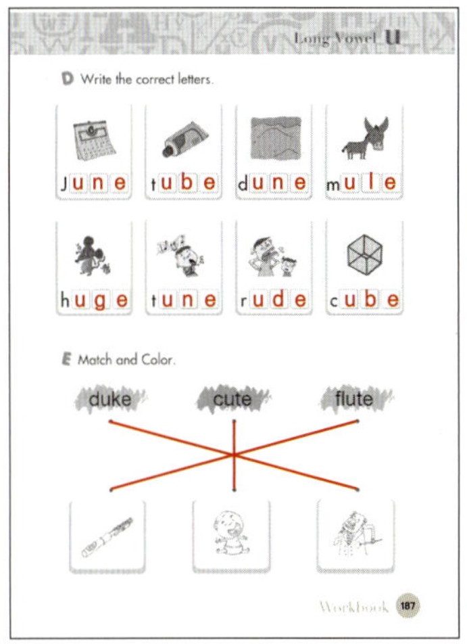

188p

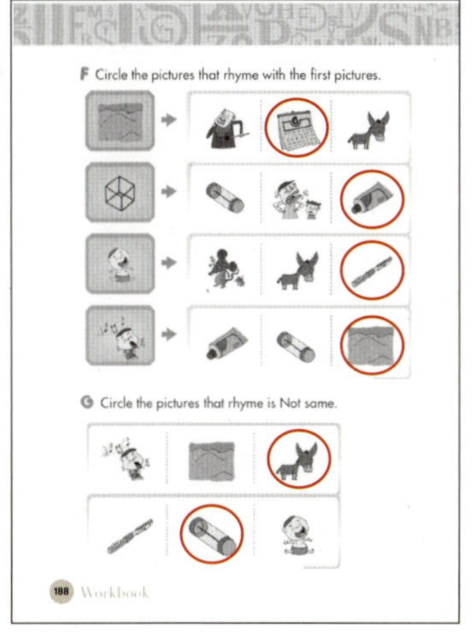

189p

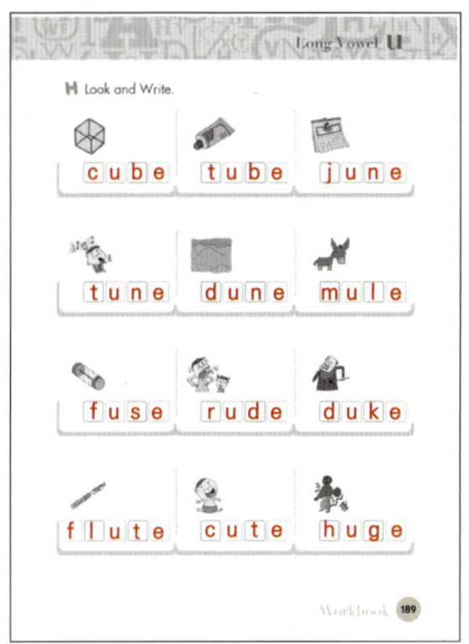

190p

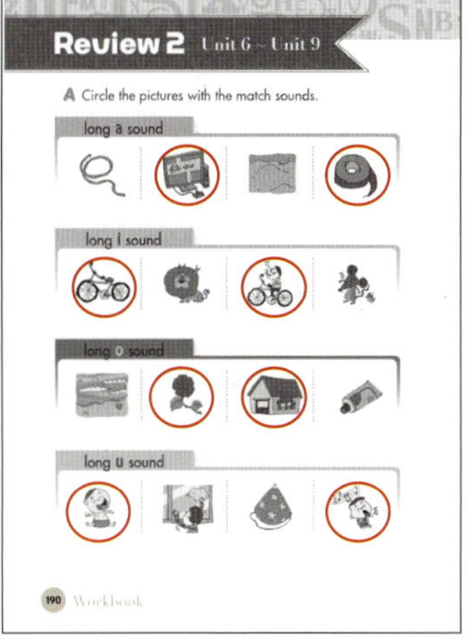

191p

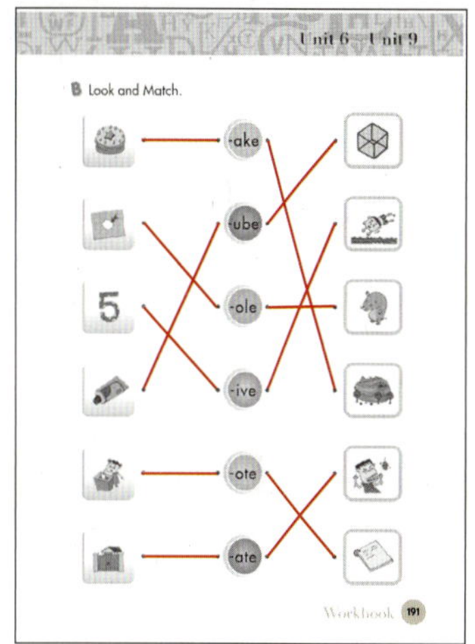

192p

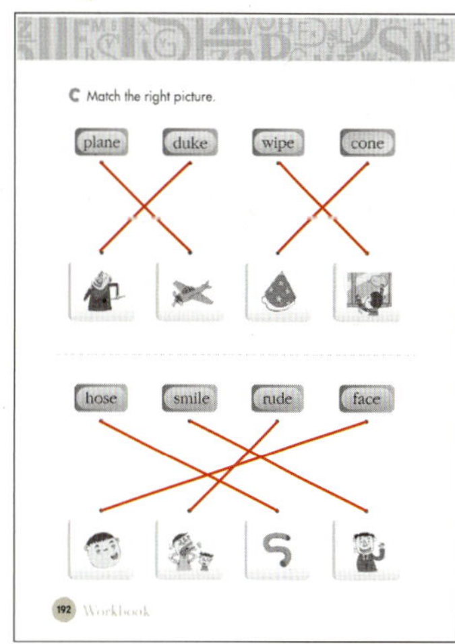

193p

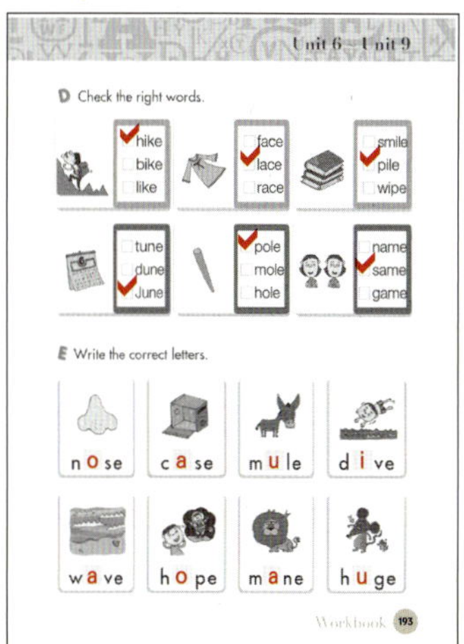

Answer Key

194p

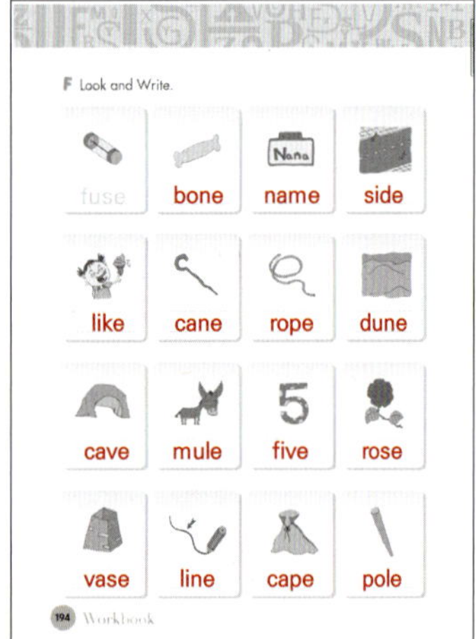

195p

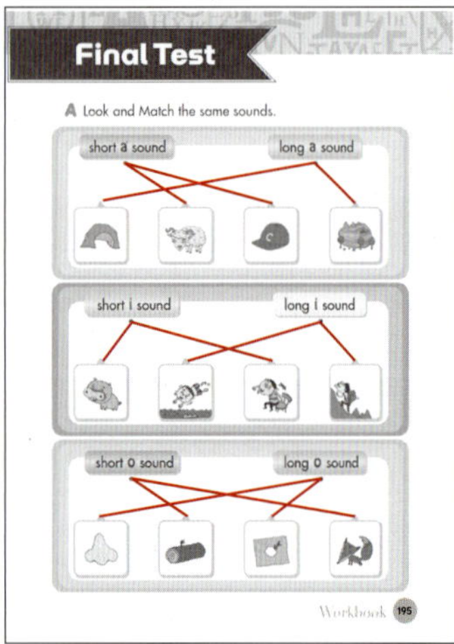

196p

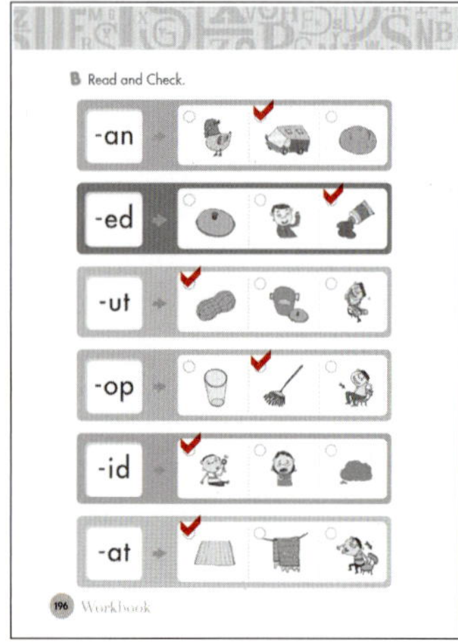

197p

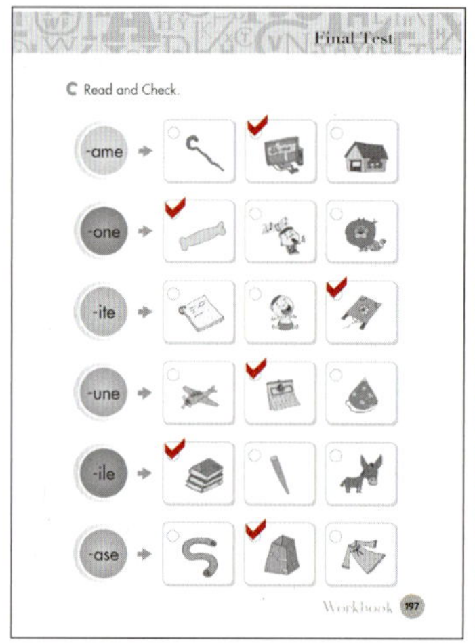

198p

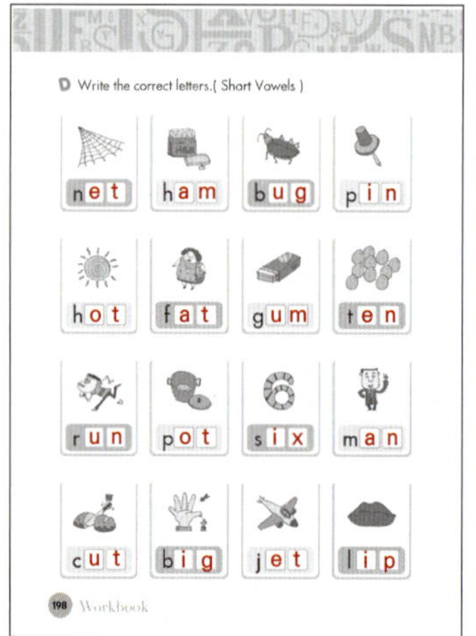

199p

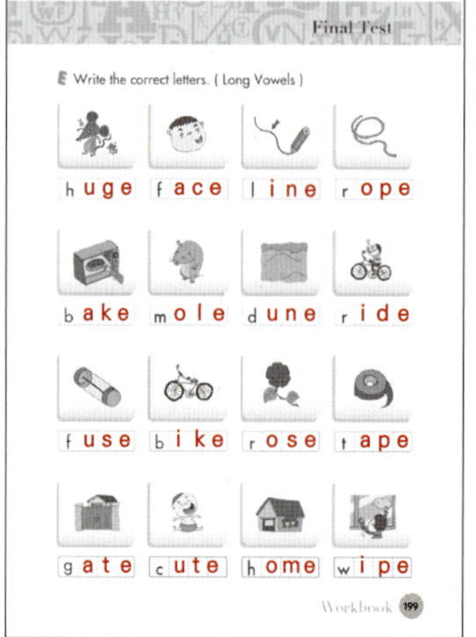

어린이 파닉스 기술을 마스터
Jump Up Phonics + Workbook시리즈

총 4권으로 구성된 Phonics 시리즈
파닉스를 단어뿐만 아니라 스토리를 통해 익힘.
신나는 챈트와 다양한 액티비티로 반복
연습리뷰와 테스트 Unit은 재미있게 복습할 수 있도록 구성

책속 부록
재미있는 활동과 놀이를 통해 영어의 기초적인 내용을 학습

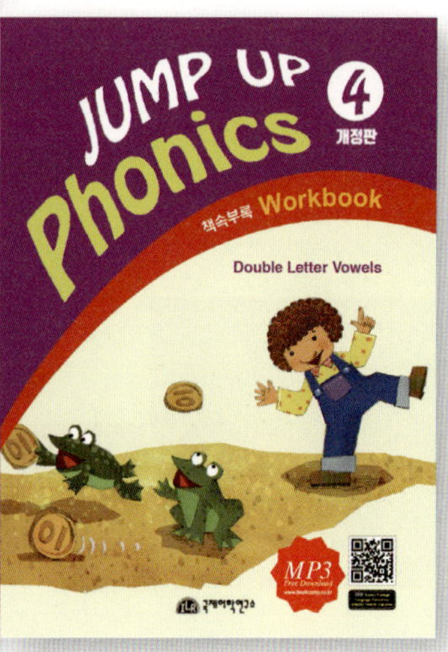